Just a Small Gathering

Volume I

Just a Small Gathering, Volume I

A Guide to Entertaining Small Groups of Family & Friends

By:
David Kershner & Scott Boles

With Wine Advice by Certified Sommelier, Donnie Austin

DJK Publishing House

Table of Contents

Acknowledgements

If it were not for the family and friends who provided us with our various experiences, this book would not have been possible.

Dave: Thank you to my wife, Tricia, for listening to my endless prattling about this book and your willingness to read revision after revision. To my daughters, Molly and Kate, thank you for at least *trying* to eat everything I put in front of you.

Scott: Thank you to my wife, Kris, for her persistent encouragement to write something based on the twenty-five plus years I spent in the kitchen. To my children, thank you for living in it for the last twenty years. And to my mother, who always made being in the kitchen enjoyable.

Preface

This book has been written by two men from vastly different backgrounds and is focused on topics that run the spectrum in terms of entertaining experience level. As such, we would like you to read our book with an open mind and have fun with the recipes and entertaining ideas. The non-recipe chapters, or narrative, deal with entertaining small groups of family and friends. They include details that you might need to think about with regard to party size and placement all the way to the guest list and the approach to the event. There is a little something in here for everyone.

The narrative chapters also contain a wealth of information pertaining to the three phases of entertaining. This information includes topics geared toward catering, hosting, and cooking. Most of the information contained in the narrative chapters has been written by Dave, with Scott adding his two-cents here and there.

The recipe chapters are where Scott really takes over and puts his stamp on this exercise. While Dave wrote the introductions to each menu chapter, and Scott and Donnie both provided their input, the recipes themselves are where Scott's experience and years of recipe cultivation and manipulation shines through.

I like to entertain but he was a professional chef and managed restaurants and resorts for over 25 years. Therefore, he wins when it comes to recipes, instructions, and technique.

Just a Small Gathering, Volume I also includes a few matrices. Matrices are a good way to convey information in an easy to understand format. A matrix is essentially a bridge for the gap that exists between, as an example, a technical and a non-technical audience. For our purposes, we have included two matrices. They are the Wine Pairing Matrix and the Meal Pairing Matrix.

The Wine Pairing Matrix is a general matrix that allows you to understand what types of wine (Merlot, Chardonnay, Pinot, etc.) go well with the main ingredient/dish (beef, chicken, fish, etc.).

The Meal Pairing Matrix provides you with 12 sample menus. These sample menus provide a main dish and a complementary appetizer, soup/salad, side, dessert, and beverage. These complementary dishes enhance the main dish in terms of similar, or possibly contrasting, flavors, textures, ingredients, etc. A supporting table provides you with cost and level of complexity indicators.

Please understand that our menus are not gospel.

By all means, chose the dishes you like and combine the flavors of different recipes to derive your own menus. These menus are meant only as a guide to get you started.

Lastly, we do want to make note that this is *not* an etiquette book. *Just a Small Gathering, Volume I* does not focus on formal party planning and, as such, we will not be discussing which fork goes where or designing the perfect table decorations.

This is a book dedicated solely to *informally* entertaining small groups of family and friends that you are welcoming into your home for a relaxing evening with some good food, drink, and companionship. There is a certain degree of familiarity and informality to the event.

Introduction

So, how did we get here?

Well, that's a loaded and interesting question. The short answer, for me, is, I like to cook, I like to garden, I like to entertain, and I like to write. I am forever a student of life. For Scott, it was the path of procrastination.

To be fair, I should point out that I have no formal background or training in the area of entertaining... and it is not my intent to become the next "Martha Stewart." But I like to entertain none-the-less. Scott is a professional chef who has worked and studied all over the United States. We are both "social butterflies" so the entertaining comes pretty natural for the two of us, but the writing and compiling has been left to me, Dave, and this book is a culmination of both our varying interests and experiences.

Due to our inquisitive nature, we both agree that the background of the story is an important part to us. Learning about the history or reasoning behind decisions and circumstances goes a long way with us in building a connection. For anything to connect, resonate, or inspire us, it needs to tell a story. It has to take the time to prepare us, the reader, with a background on the story. We live in the details!

The background could be a brief history of the town, city, state, region, or country in which the story takes place. This is mostly true for any type of book. We like it when the author takes the time to give a proper background on a character, setting, recipe, wine, etc. The background can be information about the author that goes beyond the dust jacket or communicating what inspired a particular recipe, the use of a particular ingredient, or even the reasoning behind a wine pairing. To this end, Scott and I have pondered what the appropriate background material might entail for a book geared toward informally entertaining small groups of family and friends. The following is a brief background on Scott and I and what drove us to begin the *Just a Small Gathering* series.

Dave: I, like most people, have heard, or read quotes in books and magazines, and seen movies where the term "Culinary Arts" was used. Sometimes the quotes are century's old and famous and other times not so much. I was exposed to the Culinary Arts in college when I worked as a line cook and that exposure has been invaluable. However, what really pushed me to the edge occurred in February 2009. In a nutshell, I was laid-off. I sat at home for several months and sought a new job, went on interviews, cooked simple things, cleaned, did laundry, and increased the garden's offerings. During this time, I also discovered the most wondrous thing, cooking shows.

PBS is an excellent network!

I remember watching a show on PBS titled *Made in Spain* hosted by Chef Jose Andres. He made a dish called "Pollo al Chilindron" which is basically a Spanish style chicken and tomato stew and I thought... "Well, I can cook that." Then I did! With that, my journey began in earnest. In a nod to that show, and that recipe in particular, we have included a variation of Pollo al Chilindron in the South of Border menu.

During this time on introspection, I had an epiphany. I actually enjoyed cooking and entertaining. As a result, I contemplated a career change. There are several options available to me but, in the end, I determined that I did not, in fact, want to become a chef. I don't have any great desire to work in someone else's kitchen or start a restaurant of my own. All I really wanted to do was enjoy the friendships I have and spend more quality time with family and friends.

To that end, my wife and I made a decision. When family calls and offers dinner and the pleasure of their company, you accept. No excuses. It does not matter what is being cooked or who is cooking it. It became clear that what matters, in times like these, are the relationships. Far too often we passed on these invitations because we were "too busy" and so on. Sound familiar?

I also decided to show some initiative and read the books that I owned. I coupled that knowledge with the skills acquired by watching various shows and picked up new reading materials from the library. I attended local cooking classes and demonstrations and offered to do the cooking for those family gatherings when they arose. I used these opportunities to try things I had always wanted to try.

Then finally, I coupled my passions for the kitchen and cooking with a more natural talent, writing. I started compiling a family cookbook and it slowly morphed into a premise for a blog. The blog then became the genesis for *Just a Small Gathering*. It wasn't until I proposed the idea to Scott after a Knife Skills class he taught that I fully understood just how much information there was to convey and teach others. Once Scott was on-board, the "volume" concept began to take hold because there was so much information in his head that the book would have easily been 700 pages.

Basically, that's how I got here. But that's not the entire story. We'll discuss the remainder as we get into the various sections of the book.

Scott: For me, it started in childhood. By today's standards, it is safe to say that I would have been diagnosed with ADD or ADHD and received a Ritalin prescription for my trouble but, back then, I was just described as hyperactive. As a result, my mom was always looking to stay one step ahead of me in an attempt to keep me out of trouble. So, when I was in the second grade, she started handing me box kit desserts to make. Things like Jell-O Lemon Meringue Pie or Cheesecake. I quickly tired of the kits and turned my attention towards my mom's cookbooks. Books like *The Joy of Cooking* and other Betty Crocker staples. I mostly baked in those days and didn't do much cooking. I continued to pick up kitchen knowledge, usually by trial and error, until I took a Home Economics class in high school. It was there that I realized that, maybe... just maybe, this wasn't what other families and children did.

One of our class assignments was to bake some kind of sponge cake. Of course, most everyone made an Angel Food cake. Everyone, that is, but me. I made an 8 layer Bavarian Mocha Torte! Everyone knows how to make chocolate sponge, don't they?

Apparently not.

Apparently, everyone doesn't know how to do that, nor do they know how to make a very good Angel Food cake judging from the results. My Home Economics Teacher, Mrs. Krukenburg, pulled me aside and said that I was "very different" and that maybe I should consider cooking as a profession.

"You can make a good living at cooking? I never thought of something like that." I said.

Well, she made sure I was introduced to the owner and chef of a local restaurant in our town, George Kokocedes. He had been trained at the Culinary Institute and was influential in getting me introduced to Jim

Berrini in Boston. Jim Berrini was John F. Kennedy's chef in Hyannis, MA. I'll share some of his Kennedy stories later when appropriate.

After meeting Mr. Berrini, or Mr. B. as we referred to him, we became pen pals for a couple years until I moved to Boston to study Hotel & Restaurant Management at Northeastern University and then Culinary Arts at Bunker Hill College. When I moved to Boston, I was picked up at the airport by Mr. B. and our conversation on the way to his home was some of the best stuff I ever learned about cooking and we were not anywhere near a kitchen.

What he told me was that he was going to place me in... a bakery!

"A Bakery?! How absurd! This is completely counter-productive to my plans of becoming a chef!" I silently thought to myself.

He went on to explain that, "A baker can always become a cook, but a cook can never become a baker."

In retrospect, as I look back on my career, and the careers of the people I trained, cooks, by and large, are generally lazy and will always try to take a shortcut. There are no real shortcuts in baking.

What he was trying to impart with was the knowledge that, in baking, you have to be disciplined and follow exact recipes or you might as well throw it out. A cook, on the other hand, adds a little of this and a little of that and you can usually fix, or save, a dish.

So I paid my dues, learned the art of baking, as Mr. B. instructed, and eventually moved on to train under Mr. B. and some amazingly talented chefs around the country: Arthur Buccheri of the Ritz Carlton, Maurice Laudu at Autre Chose in Cambridge, Massachusetts, and Gene Lundsford of The Mills Falls Restaurant in Newton, Massachusetts. While paying my dues in their respective kitchens, I picked up a thing known to chef's called "technique."

"Technique" to a chef is basically the chef's signature. This signature becomes the chef's calling card, or what they are known for, and it is what draws patrons time and time again. I can easily say that I have learned some great techniques from them and created my own technique. I can also say that the cooks who worked under me have also created their own techniques and it is fun, and refreshing, to see them excel and pick out some of the things that I think I may have influenced. I applied my technique as the Head or Executive Chef at The Village of Breckenridge Resort, The Velvet Cloak Inn in Raleigh, North Carolina, and the Executive Dining for Disney.

So what is technique? I guess it boils down to what comes naturally. But you would ask, "What comes naturally if I don't know how to boil water?"

Well, one of the best metaphors I have used to help others understand technique in a kitchen relates best to music. If you look at a piano, both you and I would see the standard amount of keys. If we both sat and played the piano though, the music would be completely different. I would say that this is technique. A chef's technique is simply their interpretation of musical notes where the notes are the ingredients.

Now, when I mentioned earlier, "Do what comes naturally," what I am trying to point out are the instincts you would rely on when you are not presented with enough time to think like, say, in a commercial kitchen. When you are busy and trying to cook, how do you prepare the dishes then?

When I worked for Maurice Laudu in a small, but very busy, French kitchen in Boston, he would scream at me, "La Technique! La Technique!"

What he was saying was "Don't think, just do what you know and let your talent and style flow naturally especially when you are busy."

I understand that the pressure and speed in a commercial kitchen is much more intense than in your home, but the technique you use will always be important.

Hopefully you too will take some insight from this book to create or continue to mold your own technique.

An Entertaining Background

AN ENTERTAINING BACKGROUND

So, you want to start entertaining small groups of family and friends?

I say, "Good for you!"

Here's what I've learned about entertaining... it's a three-part process.

I've learned over the years that entertaining is a different animal than just being a good cook. When you chose to entertain, you have to be one part caterer, one part host, and one part chef. This book is intended to help you begin your journey to learning aspects of all three. Don't be afraid of it! If you do it right, there is nothing that should seem, or feel, over-whelming about any of it. You may fret over whom is coming to the event (e.g. the in-laws), but the actual event should look and feel effortless and in time, with practice and learning from each event, it will become effortless. By applying what is written here, you should have a solid footing in which to begin. Besides, entertaining equals happiness... It's true!

I was listening to Colin Cowherd on a sports talk radio station as I was driving between offices one day and they were discussing something interesting. Mr. Cowherd had read an article in the NY Times that day (March 30, 2010) titled "The Sandra Bullock Trade" written by a well-known columnist named David Brooks. Mr. Brooks hypothesized, given the events regarding Sandra Bullock and her adulterous husband, "Would you exchange a tremendous professional triumph for a severe personal blow?"

She had just won an Academy Award, praised her husband in her acceptance speech, and not one week later, she learned that her husband had several extra-marital affairs... all very public tabloid fodder.

Mr. Cowherd applied the question to sports and asked a simple question: "Does money make you happy?" Given the seemingly never-ending stream of NFL players making the news for all the wrong reasons, he extrapolated that it does not. He had some interesting quotes and figures and I wish I knew the source but it went something like this...

When former professional athletes are surveyed about what they miss most about playing professionally, the highest ranked answer was always the locker room and the camaraderie of the teammates. Not the money. Not the fame. Not the limelight and newspaper clippings. It was the social interaction.

He spoke of families/couples that entertain being happier than those that do not because of the social interaction. He had a figure that said something like 20% of comedians and novelists are on anti-depressants due to the rigors of the road and isolation; whereas, the general population of America averages about 10%-12%. (I would like to note that I am not on anti-depressants!) He also noted that American troops in the middle of a war zone, away from their families, being shot at, with the specter of death around any given corner have an overall depression rate of only 8%.

Why are American troops showing a lower percentage of depression than the entire population?

It's the same answer as the professional athlete, the camaraderie of teammates.

So, in an effort to keep from being depressed, or in an effort to pull you out of a funk... you should have people over and entertain!

The proof is in the figures.

Now that you know that entertaining is therapeutic, it is important to point out that it's not really as hard as you may have made it out to be. Believe it or not, almost everybody has done some form of entertaining during the course of his or her life.

Ever had anyone over for the big game?

Ever had movie night with a group of friends?

Don't look now but, you were entertaining small groups of family and friends.

For me, entertaining came to pass because of several things. Firstly, I was looking for a way to give my wife a respite from the daily monotony of being a schoolteacher, wife, and mother to two young girls. I wanted her to have conversations with adults, plain and simple. I figured that if I did all the setup, cooking, and clean up, and managed to keep the girls out of her hair for an hour or two, she could spend some quality time with family and friends.

Secondly, I wanted to prove to myself that I could entertain and have a good time while doing so. Once I turned my attention toward making sure guests were having a good time, instead of focusing solely on myself, entertaining became a much more worthwhile experience... and it made my wife happy to see I was actually growing up!

And lastly, entertaining is a bit of an homage to my life, places I've been, things I've seen, and things I've experienced.

The summers of my youth were spent exploring the hardwood forests of the Shenandoah Valley and touring Revolutionary and Civil War battlefields in Northern Virginia. While "exploring," my brothers and I would attempt to apply knowledge gained from our Boy Scout manuals. During the summers, our parents would ship the four of us off to summer camp, Scout Camp, or we would go on vacation to Chincoteague Island off the coast of Virginia with another family.

When on Chincoteague, we would be handed a half of a pack of chicken and a crab pot with the instructions of "go catch dinner." So we rode our bikes to the marsh water, baited the traps, chucked them in the water, and went to the water park until lunch. Come lunchtime, we went and emptied the pots, returned the crabs to our parents, ate lunch, and received the other half of the chicken. We rode back and re-baited the pots, went and played around the island, or went back to the water park, until dinnertime. At dinnertime we collected the crabs, and the pots, and returned both to our parents. Times were different then. *Deadliest Catch* this was not.

Although, I do have a confession to make... we played with our food. We would practice our jump shots with live crab and boiling pots of water. There were many impressions of the wicked witch as the crabs entered the pot of water... "I'm meelllttttiiing!" There is no need to call PETA. I was a child. I know what I did was wrong and I'm sorry.

Moving on... once my dad retired from the Navy, we moved even further south to Southern Pines, NC. Southern Pines is right next to a little town you may have heard of, if you happen to be a golf fan, called Pinehurst, NC.

The pace of life in Southern Pines/Pinehurst is slow. Nothing is done around there with any great sense of urgency and they like it that way. It is safe to say that when my wife took a teaching position there after college, she experienced a bit of a culture shock. We didn't meet up with friends and go to bars to hang out, nobody was ever in a hurry to be anywhere in particular; punctuality was recommended but not required...

kind of like a speed limit in that regard. Anyway, once you've met my wife, and spend five minutes with her, you'll know and understand that the pace and lifestyle emitted from that sleepy little Hamlet was completely foreign to her.

O.K. I'll say it, she's a Yankee! She's more of a Midwestern Yankee but a Yankee all the same. That's why we complement each other so well... that's my side of the story at any rate.

As I was saying, where I grew up, we didn't spend time in bars and restaurants. We went to each other's homes for BBQ's... or if you happen to be dating the girl from the other side of the tracks; you went with her family to Pinehurst Country Club for Sunday brunch after church. It's all very "Leader of the Pack" at this point so I'll move on... This isn't an autobiography.

My best friend growing up lived on, what you might call, a "Gentlemen's Estate." Thirty acres, or so, of hedgerow divided pastures owned by an avid outdoorsman. The house resembles a giant hunting lodge. Stacked stone, stucco, cedar shake roof, and rough-cut lumber everywhere. It was a great place to learn about the outdoors and I wouldn't trade it for the world. On this little slice of farmland, my friend's parents had a freezer full of various meats from the family's hunting pursuits and I was exposed to it all.

I have eaten buffalo, red stag, venison, boar, duck, goose, dolphin fish, rainbow trout, largemouth bass, you name it, if it can be hunted or caught on a line it was in the freezer and I ate it. Now, not everyone down South is as avid outdoorsmen as this family but my point here is this; it exposed me to other things beside the traditional hamburgers and hotdogs you would typically find at a backyard BBQ.

Also, the term "BBQ" in this part of North Carolina refers more to a lovely colloquialism known as, "the pig pickin'."

In most of North Carolina, the only BBQ served is called Eastern North Carolina BBQ. Basically, it's pulled pork with a vinegar-based sauce. My wife is now a pulled pork snob because anything other than Eastern North Carolina BBQ and she'll be polite but, she won't enjoy it.

Here is a short little story to give you a little background into my sheltered little life.

Very early on in our relationship, we drove north to Ohio to visit her family. The family decided we would eat out at some dive they all seemed to enjoy and thought I might appreciate as well. I noticed they had BBQ in the menu and ordered it. My wife gently whispered, "It's not what you think it is. You're not going to like it."

"Oh, I'll be fine... BBQ is BBQ." I replied.

Did you know that there is such a thing as Northern BBQ and Southern BBQ?

I didn't.

I was unaware of this crack in the fabric of the universe and all I can say is that someone needs to sew the crack back together because Northern BBQ is most definitely an acquired taste that I will never acquire.

That plate was promptly sent back.

Would you believe they smothered the pork in some weird thick red sauce goop? A trained chef couldn't have identified it as even being pork!

I've wandered a bit off topic here but I think we have an understanding now. I was exposed to many types of food and presentation styles and all of it has been incorporated in how I approach entertaining small groups of family and friends. Anything I didn't acquire during my "formative years," I gained by watching others and trying things on my own. That's right... I'm self-taught.

I like to think that I subscribe to, what is considered, a more European approach towards entertaining – which is very much in tune with the slower Southern approach I mentioned previously. This isn't to say that we here in the United States don't attribute many of these qualities to our entertaining, quite the contrary. To me, entertaining friends and family is a way to spend time with the people I care about and consider friends and loved ones. Entertaining small groups of people is more about the forging and strengthening of relationships whether they are familial or other. As such, this is the approach I have taken to entertaining small gatherings of family and friends.

The food served plays an important part, of course, but the entire event is comprised of much, much more. It's about the conversation; it's about the bonding that can take place over shared events in life that no one, until the event, knew the other was going through. People share things about themselves more readily when there is lower stress, smaller groups, and a mood that lends itself to introspection.

The following story depicts what can happen if you have an open mind toward small gatherings and a willingness to be spontaneous.

Some time ago, my wife and I happened upon an occasion to put the crux of my approach to entertaining into full practice. Our daughters had swim practice after school and a friend's daughter is also in the class. The other couples older daughter was taking part in an "invention convention" downtown and they didn't want to make their younger daughter suffer through the event so we took the youngest daughter home with us. We told the other couple not to rush, as their daughter was welcome to stay as long as necessary and that we would feed her dinner. What happened next proves everything I have written, or will write, regarding the premise behind entertaining.

The other couple, and their daughter, finished setting up the daughter's invention presentation faster than anticipated so my wife simply invited them to stay and eat with us. I offered up to my wife that I could go and get some basil and some heavy cream to make my yummy Provencal Pistou Pasta but she declined. She stated very matter of fact, that we will eat whatever is in the house. She quickly whipped up some traditional spaghetti with red sauce and meatballs, a basic salad with pine nuts, and sent me for a fresh baguette. There was a bottle of wine chilling for the last few days in the fridge so we served that with the meal.

The entire meal was as relaxed and stress free as any meal I can quickly recall. There was no scurrying around or panic regarding the state of the house because it was fairly kept up all week long. The two couples laughed and talked and shared stories and all four girls were complete angels. The children talked about their individual days at school, how things were going in class or with classmates, excitement over the upcoming ballet recital in a few weeks... we simply enjoyed the pleasure of each other's company.

This meal was an excellent example of what entertaining is all about really. It isn't necessarily all about the food. It's more about providing a comfortable environment in which to strengthen relationships, converse, share, and laugh. I say, "Kudos" to my wife for the educating lesson. Plus, if you are open to spontaneity, you can quickly find yourself having a great deal of fun when you were least expecting it.

Now, in addition to these lessons from my wife, I have read a lot of books, watched a lot of cooking shows, and begrudgingly, decorating shows. Scott and I have applied a great deal of knowledge into the events that we have held. Even today, we have learned something from each and every event. Sometimes it was the discovery that something just isn't worth the effort and sometimes you hit on that one thing that binds the event together as a shared experience among the guests.

This is what we hope to convey here with this guide to entertaining small groups of family and friends.

Channeling Your Inner Caterer

CHANNELING YOUR INNER CATERER

If you want to begin entertaining small gatherings of friends and family, you will need to channel your inner caterer. There's no two ways about it. Pick a style or motif and go with it. I am going to try and place a clear distinction between the decoration aspects, which I am deeming "host duty," and the items used to set the table for each event.

For the catering aspects, I have acquired a collection of items that we use time and again when we entertain. My preferences lean more to rustic or antique items as opposed to say, modern. I enjoy the occasional visit to a flea market, yard sale, and antique shop in search of those items that may further complement the things I already own. These items could be wine charms, a sideboard, hearty outdoor furniture, etc. However, too much rustic can be overwhelming as well; therefore, I have limited my rustic motif to my serveware.

An Arsenal of "Wares"

With all of the terms used for the items that make up a table setting, it can quickly become confusing, or even, frustrating. There are terms like "serveware," "dinnerware," "drinkware," "stemware," etc. So here's a quick primer:

Serveware derives its name from its intended purpose, which is the serving of the food. This includes your pitchers, large serving platters, and bowls but can also include the pot or pan it was cooked in. Some folks refer to it as "serving ware" (shown as two-words compared to one-word) and I have seen it both ways in print so I'm going with "serveware" (one-word).

Dinnerware is what the dinner is actually served to your guests on, or in. This means dinner plates, salad plates, and bowls. Some people also lump dinner plates and salad plates into flatware due to its low profile, or flat, nature. We will dispense with that flip-flopping ambiguity here though.

Flatware consists of eating utensils like forks, knives, and spoons.

Drinkware can be an all-encompassing term for some people as it is, at times, used to refer to all glasses or cups used to serve beverages. This general definition sometimes includes wine glasses but I'll have none of that vagary here either. Drinkware, to me, is any cup or glass that does not have a stem. Therefore, wine glasses are not considered glassware.

Stemware consists of wine glasses. Wine glasses are classified as stemware for a reason... because they have a stem.

And finally, as if there weren't enough information to understand, four of these terms roll up into one, more general, term known as tableware. If you are referring to the whole place setting (i.e. flatware, dinnerware, glassware, and stemware) then use of the term tableware is more appropriate.

SERVEWARE

My serveware is different from everything else in the house and nothing matches. This is done by design. I prefer my serveware to be eclectic because when it is placed on the table, your attention is immediately drawn to it. It is

a centerpiece of sorts. None of our serveware is perfectly flat like the dinnerware. It is full of colors, dips, pits, and ridges and is as far removed from the perfect mass produced serveware we received at our wedding as possible. They

look like they were actually crafted by an imperfect human being on a potter's wheel. We still have those *Pottery Barn* platters and bowls and

use them from time-to-time but it just doesn't say, "Look at me," when we use them. If you have, or can acquire, enough serveware, three to five pieces of varying size, you should be all right. If you have a *TJ Maxx* nearby, I would consider wandering through there. The shopping experience can be inexpensive and entertaining all in one.

DINNERWARE

All of the plates, bowls, and cups that comprise our dinnerware are from our wedding registry and they came from *Pottery Barn* as well, the PB White style to be exact. It has a classic look and lines that are not ostentatious and do not contain any patterns or gold or silver inlays.

They are just plain ol' white plates. Our formal dinnerware contains a gold inlay so it can't be washed in the dishwasher. I am not really sure why we registered for something we never use but we did, just

like everyone else I imagine, and we received it as a gift. To be honest, I think those plates are still boxed up after our move from Charlotte, North Carolina to Columbus, Ohio almost decade ago.

I feel like I should be receiving some sort of endorsement for mentioning *Pottery Barn* so much but I need to mention one more thing. *Pottery Barn* started carrying something called "Caterer's Boxes." Inside these handy little boxes is usually twelve of whatever you are purchasing.

For instance, I purchased a Caterer's Box of dinner plates. I needed the extra plates because I wanted to do a five-course meal for six adults and didn't want to have to do dishes in the middle of the event. They also offer Caterer's Boxes for salad plates, soup bowls, and cereal bowls. I only mention it here because the plates in the Caterer  Box are, almost, a perfect match for our everyday dinnerware. So I got lucky in that regard.

If you are going to host events, you will need enough dinnerware to serve the meal to the guests (i.e. Caterer's Box). If it is informal, or possibly outside, consider recycled, or recyclable, paper or plastic products because, let's face it, plates break.

FLATWARE

Our flatware, also commonly referred to as silverware, is in the same wheelhouse as the dinnerware, pretty much plain. I think we found them at *Wal-Mart*. Plain is a good thing because it is inexpensive to replace the whole set if pieces get lost or damaged by that vicious dishwasher... which is second cousin to the sock monster residing in the clothes dryer!

It goes without saying that you also need enough flatware for your guests to actually get the food into their mouths. I like a good weight, or heft, to my flatware. Get what feels comfortable to you.

DRINKWARE

Our drinkware is a mismatch of different styles and thicknesses. Originally, everything came from, I dare say it again, *Pottery Barn*. But, we have broken enough glasses over the years that we bought new thicker highball (tall) glasses and returned to the "apothecary table" store to purchase new tumblers (medium) and juice glasses (small) to replace the broken ones.

"Apothecary table" store. That's funny if you saw the episode of "Friends" where Phoebe goes to the dark side of commercialism and purchases an apothecary table from *Pottery Barn*. It's a classic.

Anyway, we have twelve of each and use them for entertaining and everyday use.

STEMWARE

Our stemware is plain as well, come to think of it. We have eight glasses for white wine and eight glasses for red wine. You can tell the difference between a white wine glass and red wine glass by the shape and width of mouth of the glass. The bigger wider glasses are the red wine glasses.

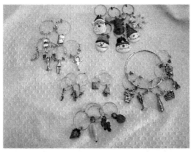

Also, we add a personal touch with colorful and classic looking wine charms. The wine charms are used to help guests identify which glass is theirs if left unattended on a table our counter top. The wine charms are placed at the bottom, or around, the stem. It's a simple thing, really, but the guests can get a kick out of choosing their wine charm especially if you can find sets that are colorful or fit a specific season or theme.

That covers the basic of what you need on the table for people to eat the meal. Now let's talk about tables and chairs and the rest of it.

TABLES & CHAIRS

I, like most people, do the majority of my entertaining during the warmer summer months when everyone can come and go inside and out without fear of freezing to death. So as to not take away any table space for diners, we purchased a folding table. However, we use this folding table for two purposes depending on the season and reason for the event.

If it is a sit down type of gathering, I'll butt it up against the existing dining room table as an extension of sorts to increase seating capacity. With a tablecloth over both no one really notices or minds.

If it is a summertime, outdoor, or potluck style event, I'll place the table against a wall in the dining room near the back door. Guests can then use the table to place whatever dish they have brought with them.

The rectangular six-foot long folding table was acquired from *Target* but you can find them most of the time in any big box store.

We also have patio furniture we use but, until recently, it was comprised of a four foot round table and it was difficult to put more than four or five people around it with all of their plates, cups, bowls, etc. Since more than a decade had passed since we purchased patio furniture, it took some doing, but, we acquired a six-foot long oval shaped patio table in the same style as the original furniture. By increasing the size and changing the shape it allows more guests to sit at the table when dining outdoors. We'll discuss outdoor planning in a little bit.

Eventually, though, I would like to get around to purchasing folding chairs but, until then, we borrow the neighbors patio chairs or the in-laws folding chairs when needed. Times are tough on a lot of people so there should be no shame in asking to borrow a few... especially if they are on the guest list. However, if you ever want to borrow them again, return them in as good a shape as when you got them or replace it  if you, or a guest, broke it. Unless the guest is the owner in which case it is their fault and you are off the hook.

We'll discuss outdoor dining and tables and chairs more in the host section later on.

> *Fun Factoid: Did you know that you can inquire, and possibly purchase, display items from department stores?*

I'm not talking about the coffee maker that was on display for a reduced cost. No, I am referring to the actual decorations, tables, and display pieces.

I spent about a month trying to acquire a 4 x 8 teak table I saw in *Sears*. They had six of them being used as props but, in the end, they

couldn't part with even one of them. It never hurts to ask. The worst they can say is "no." Being told "no" doesn't hurt when that's what you were expecting them to say to begin with. It's when they say, "Yes" that you need to have your wits about you and negotiate a decent price for the piece. Be prepared to have them tell you the piece can't be picked up until the end of the season though.

TABLECLOTHS & NAPKINS

Now let's talk about tablecloths and napkins. Technically, these items may fall under the heading of "host duty" but every good caterer I've seen provided them. I like tablecloths like I like my serveware... eclectic.

Who says you have to go with a plain white tablecloth?

Yes, they are easy to clean with bleach but a white tablecloth also conveys formality. You are entertaining family and friends. It's your house not a five-star restaurant.

Live a little!

Put some color and design work into your tablecloth selection. My wife will probably keel over when she reads this but color isn't something to be afraid of.

Here's a little story about color gone wrong.

As a High School Biology teacher, my wife gets Spring Break off. On one such occasion, she chose to fly to Columbus to visit family during her break. This was pre-children so last minute flights with odd arrival and departure times were not that big a deal. While she was gone, I thought I would surprise her by painting the bedroom the same color as her favorite pillows, which were this satin maroon color.

So I headed to the big box home improvement store, pillow in hand, and proceeded to work with the "color specialist" to match the pillow. We decided on the color, he mixed the paint, and I returned home with my two-gallons of paint and commenced with the preparation of the surprise. The painting was slow going as all four walls were covered in this popcorn texture garbage which made cutting in the walls, corners, ceiling, doors, and windows next to unbearable but I got it done before she returned. I thought she would be so happy and surprised and proud of me but I tragically misjudged her reaction.

I received the lecture or a lifetime for about thirty-minutes upon her discovery that the room was not, in fact, maroon as I had thought it was, but rather a more emboldened hue of fire-engine red! It was at this point that I was informed, rather emphatically by her, that I was going to be the one playing dumb when the landlord did the final walk through or I was going to be the one repainting the room white if he didn't buy my "dumb act."

Morale of the story: Embrace the color of life… but display it as tastefully as possible.

You can also use tablecloths and runners and napkins as an excuse to learning sewing and embroidery techniques.

What?

Yes, I am a grown man and I just used the words "sewing" and "embroidery techniques." I told you, I reluctantly watched decorating shows.

If you have never lost a button off of a shirt, jacket, a pair shorts, or trousers then, guess what, if you put the button back on, instead of throwing them out, you were sewing! It's not just for Betsy Ross I tell you!

Now, I grant you, making your own runner or any other item is a little more involved than sewing on a button but, it could be fun. Give it a try. I once worked with a guy that used cross-stitching as a relaxation technique. He actually did some phenomenal work. It was very impressive to me for the sole reason that I can't do it… but back to the topic.

If you can't find a tablecloth or runner to your liking, make one yourself. Whatever you do, have the napkins complement the table setting. Clashing colors or patterns are not ideal, obviously, so if you don't have an eye for this type of discernment, entrust the task to a spouse or close friend or family member. Have this individual assist you in finding matching patterns or complementary colors.

In our house, my wife sets out the girls clothes everyday because I cannot be counted on to send them to school in outfits that don't clash in some manner. I don't have the eye for it but, thankfully, she does. The girls are even getting better at it. I'll come downstairs for work and the oldest will either give me the "stink eye" or the thumbs up. The stink eye says, "Really? You're going to wear that to work?" When I see this I simply turn around and try again.

COSTS

When it comes to entertaining, you can keep individual event costs down by borrowing items from friends, neighbors, and family. If friends or family are getting rid of items, offer to take them off of their hands and put them back to good use. *Craig's List* and *eBay* are also viable resources, as are, garage sales, estate sales, and a relaxing weekend spent antiquing.

Seriously, walking around dusty stores full of someone else's useless stuff can be relaxing. I find it relaxing at any rate. That is, when the girls are with their grandparents and it is just my wife and I. They tend to add to the stress level by handling extremely expensive things that I have neither the funds nor the inclination to purchase.

You can also reduce your overall entertaining costs by acquiring the various items (tables, chairs, tableware, serveware, decorations, etc.) over a period of time. Nobody ever graduated from college, got their first job, and blew their first paycheck on tableware. In the end, acquire items over time and reuse, recycle, and repurpose older items.

Discovering Your Inner Host

DISCOVERING YOUR INNER HOST

Entertaining small groups of family and friends can be a worthwhile and rewarding experience. However, as Newton tells us, for every action, there is an equal, and opposite, reaction. Entertaining can be expensive, time consuming, and a complete and utter pain.

The trick is finding the middle ground.

That middle ground comes with time and practice but will eventually lead you to be cost conscience, efficient, and a part of the gathering instead of just the host offering abbreviated "hellos." Spending the evening "working rooms" and scurrying back and forth to the kitchen to finish preparing a meal you most likely won't get to enjoy doesn't make for a good time for you, the host.

By entertaining smaller groups, you get to be a part of the gathering, the conversation, and the event. You can move the conversation along or offer your two cents on a particular topic instead of just hearing portions of conversations as you work your way between rooms.

In order to properly prepare for a small gathering of family or friends, you need to consider several factors. You need to plan for the: who, what, where, when, why, and how of the event.

Let's begin by discussing the factors that go into deriving the guest list.

Guest List

You wouldn't think it, but the guest list can require just as much thought as the theme or the meal itself. I tend to base my invite list on several factors. Some of these factors include:

Reason for the Event
Time and Effort
Size
Seating Capacity
Meal Offering
Personal Preferences

Each of these factors, while seemingly independent of one another, is, in fact, related to the others. I will try not to blur the lines between them too much.

Reason for the Event

If the reason for the event is because you wanted to try something upscale, you might want to reconsider inviting your binge drinking college buddies. The time and effort that goes in to creating the event is better served on guests who would appreciate the theme and the associated meal. Now, if you plan on grilling in the back yard and are willing to provide a keg of something, then by all means invite the keg standers and beer-bongers. They would appreciate this event!

The reason for the event can be anything you want it to be. Son/daughter had an accomplishment of some merit? Include the child in the planning of an event to celebrate. Got a tax refund and spent it on a big screen TV? Invite friends over to watch "the game." Entertaining doesn't always have to be about a celebration or showing off your latest acquisition. Entertain when you feel you haven't had enough adult interaction lately or when you have acquired a recipe or two or three that you want to try. Entertain when you feel the need to spend time with family and friends. Entertaining is a personal thing so the reason for an event can be as varied as your interests.

Be creative!

TIME AND EFFORT

I touched on this briefly but here are some other things to consider in this category: if guests truly knew the time, effort, and financial aspects of an event, you can rest assured that, they would be offering to assist the host each and every time.

As an example, should you discover on a Thursday afternoon that your plans to go out on Saturday evening fell through, and you want to invite people to your home, given the amount of time remaining before Saturday evening, you might want to scale back your effort and plan something a little simpler. Entertaining is supposed to be fun and rewarding and worthwhile. Trying to throw something together, complete with guest list, theme, and prep in two days may be more than a bit taxing. Unless it is an extremely informal pot-luck styled event, I'd take the weekend off and plan something for the following weekend.

As your family grows, so will your circle of friends. As your circle grows, you will be in a better position to reduce costs when entertaining. We have friends that we are so close with that we have "pajama and leftover nights." That's when everyone gets to wear his or her sweats or PJ's and everyone brings whatever leftovers are in the fridge. Think of it as a poor man's potluck. It's fun. Try it and see for yourself.

You can also reduce costs by actually having a potluck and ask guests  to bring a dish big enough to serve 6 to 8 people (or however many you think it needs to feed). Tell them the main course you are providing and ask them to bring something specific or something that you think will complement the main dish. It's your event. Here's the key though, if you are going to entertain in this manner, you have to reconcile yourself with the art of delegating.

SIZE

The size, or scope, of the event will almost always be the determining factor when it comes to determining the number of guests. The size of the event may even drive the event outdoors. From there you will need to take in to account things like lot size, front or back yard, shade, busy/quiet street, canopies, seating for the elderly, pregnant, and disabled.

The last statement is the key in determining the size of the event. Seating capacity and, to a lesser extent, theme, or reason for the event, will also factor into determining your guest list.

SEATING CAPACITY

Let's discuss table and space limitations for a moment... because before you can be a host, you need to know how many people can fit in, and out, of your home.

Will the event be indoors or outdoors?

Is there any shade?

INDOORS

Let's say, for the sake of argument, that it is the dead of winter and you want to have people over. Take a look around and see just how many people you can host comfortably indoors. If you are in a cramped apartment, chances are that the majority of your friends are also in a cramped apartment. As such, they should understand if the guest list has to be limited. Just be aware of your surroundings and scope your guest list accordingly.

In our home, we can have a gathering where people are milling about comfortably with a maximum of 4-6 couples and their children - we have a spare bedroom that is setup as a play room to herd all of the children into so, yeah parents! That being said, if I want to serve a sit down meal, this number, for us, is reduced by half due to the size of the table and the available seating capacity at the table. This is true even when we feed the guests in shifts with the children being fed first, followed by the adults.

Needless to say, we are currently on the lookout for a table with a larger seating capacity.

OUTDOORS

Now, if you are looking to host a larger engagement, you need to survey your property. If you look at your property (lot size, configuration,

fencing, gate locations, etc.), how many people can you comfortably accommodate and provide seating opportunities?

By seating opportunities, I am referring to places where the elderly, pregnant, or disabled can sit for long stretches of time. Most people do not enjoy standing for an entire party so seating scattered throughout the area is wise.

Do you have a sturdy folding table(s)?

Any extra chairs (folding or other) stuffed in the basement or attic?

Target, or one of the big box stores, carries a nice six-foot folding table for about $30.00 - $50.00 depending on the size. Extra chairs can be had at garage sales, *Craig's List*, *eBay*, etc. Also, as a side note, depending on the type of event you want to host, consider buying a roll of butcher paper (3 ft. wide) to use as a tablecloth and provide a basket of crayons for guests to doodle with... everyone likes to doodle.

SHADE

How much natural shade is provided in your yard by the foliage from trees, bushes, and shrubs?

What time of day is the event being held?

The reason I point this out is because depending on the time of day, you may, or may not, have more or less shade depending on the time of year. Prior to announcing your event, go outside during the time span of when you think you would like to host your event.

How much shade is available?

What and where is it shaded?

If the answers are "not much," consider purchasing a 10x10 canopy from a sporting goods store or online. I suggest the 10x10 size because it allows you to place a small round table and four chairs under the canopy

and most everyone seated there will be shaded in some regard. If your yard has some shading, consider placing a seating area there so guests can venture out of the sun. If your yard is totally shaded,

place the seating anywhere you like. However, if your yard is totally shaded and the weather forecast calls for cooler temperatures, consider two things:

Consider moving the event to portions of your property that could potentially hold some sunshine or;

Consider holding the event both inside and out so your guests can warm up indoors if they haven't dressed appropriately.

Better still, there is also a third option, if you own a fire pit, consider placing a fire in the fire pit to keep guests warm. (NOTE: if you chose the fire pit option, remember to consider your guests with small children.)

If the function is a neighborhood thing and the street is quiet, I would then consider the front yard as an option. Also, many cities and suburbs allow for temporary street closures for neighborhood block parties provided the requested street is not a major thoroughfare (or artery) or an emergency back-up road.

Again, will there be children?

If so and street parking is allowed, consider parking your car in front of your driveway (assuming there is a driveway). This will effectively block off the driveway for the children to play there with chalk and jump ropes and ride bikes and big wheels and stuff.

Don't have those things?

Ask the parents of the children to bring toys for the children to play with outside.

Do you know anyone with a slip-n-slide?

Consider borrowing one for the kids to use during the party. Better still; invite the owners to attend and ask them to bring the children's items with them. Kill two birds with one stone. It really depends on the occasion for the event as to what you do to accommodate the families with children for an outdoor party.

OUTDOOR MISCELLANEOUS

Prior to the event, do yourself a favor and address the backyard. Mow, weed-eat, and remove any dangerous items/implements that may injure a guest.

For our family, as an example, we felt it was important to address our deteriorating brick patio.

"How does landscaping fall under being a host," you ask?

Well, I'll tell you... who wants to come to a house where the bricks are lying in wait to twist an ankle or trip some unsuspecting toddler?

Basically, it looked horrible and we were sick of it. So we saved our money and addressed the issue.

To be fair, my mother-in-law installed the patio as a form of physical therapy after falling down the stairs and breaking her wrist quite badly. "Grandma Sa," as our girls know her, was told by the doctors that she would only regain 50%-60% mobility in her wrist. She works as a dental hygienist so that answer was not going to fly.

So, in order to strengthen her wrist and regain lost mobility and dexterity, she had a pallet of brick delivered. She moved the brick to the back yard and then she sat there with a pile of brick and a garden trowel. She proceeded to dig out the grass, drop in some sand, and then install a brick. She did this one brick at a time with one hand!

Now, once we bought the house from her, and began using the patio with greater frequency, the bricks began to sink and spread until you have the minefield of danger I previously described. The patio is a focal point in our entertaining so by addressing this issue, we cleaned up an eyesore and a hazard.

Another eyesore we addressed was the 50-year-old chain link fence that surrounded our back yard. We opted to replace it with a cedar fence because we felt it was more in line with our tastes than the pre-fabricated sections of wooden fence that are available at home improvement stores.

In an odd little twist, we only owned two of the three sides of the

fence that abutted our yard. We had

previously received permission from our

neighbor to the rear but we unfortunately

put the fence off for so long that the

owner of the house had changed. When

we called to ask if it was OK to replace his fence the answer he gave us

was quite shocking and not at all what we were expecting. In a nutshell,

his words were, and I quote, "My house, my property, my fence. Don't

touch my fence!"

Umm, we weren't really sure what to do with that so I explained it a

different way. "We would like to replace your rusted 50-year-old chain

link fence with a new 6 ft. cedar privacy

fence." Unfortunately, we were met with

the same response.

I had a manager once that imparted

me with some sage advice. He said, "Not

making a decision is still making a decision and everybody is different.

Different isn't bad, different is just different."

C'est le Vie.

Regardless, these are all just ideas for what you can do with your

outdoor space.

Who knew that there was so much to consider when it comes to the setting, seating, shading, indoor, outdoor, front yard, backyard...

MEAL OFFERING

Here's where you address the finicky eaters and the guests with allergies.

If you really want to serve a fish, or a seafood themed meal, why would you invite people with aversions to fish?

Or better still, why are you inviting the people with a specific type of allergy to an event where something is served containing the ingredient that they are highly allergic to?

Do you just want to see them use their epi pen?

Then there are those potential guests that still hold on to preconceived notions from childhood of what something looks, smells, or tastes like. I call these people my "green eggs and ham" club. I have, however, on occasion, gone out of my way to fix something for the "green eggs and ham" club member because the spouse is someone who would really appreciate and enjoy the meal being served. So, in an effort to include everyone, I make something on the side for the spouse.

You can use friends and family members with allergies as guinea pigs as well. If you have someone who has, say, a gluten allergy, then try and find a gluten free recipe and invite them over to try it. Simple. They get to be involved and everyone still gets to eat.

MEAL PLANNING ESTIMATES

We have spent a great of time explaining the small informal gathering in terms of a sit down meal. However, not all small gatherings are sit-down meals. If this happens to be the case for you and your future

 event, then perhaps the following table will be of some assistance. If you are planning an event, and by "event" we mean a small gathering, that contains more of a buffet of finger foods, these

planning estimates may be worth considering. Events like these may be along the lines of a graduation party, tailgate, family reunion, holiday celebration, etc.

# of Guests	Meats (3 oz. per guest)	Cheese (1 1/2 oz. per guest)	Salads (4 oz. per guest)	Bread (3 slices per guest)	Rolls (1-2 per guest)	Chips (2 oz. per guest)	Dips (1 oz. Per guest)
4	3/4 lb.	6 oz.	1 lb.	12 slices	4 - 8	8 oz.	4 oz.
8	1 1/2 lb.	3/4 lb.	2 lb.	24 slices	8 - 16	1 lb.	8 oz.
12	2 1/4 lb.	1 1/8 lb.	3 lb.	36 slices	1 - 2 dz.	1 1/2 lb.	12 oz.
16	3 lb.	1 1/2 lb.	4 lb.	48 slices	1 1/2 - 3 dz.	2 lb.	1 lb.
24	4 1/2 lb.	2 1/4 lb.	5 lb.	72 slices	2 - 4 dz.	3 lb.	1 1/2 lb.
32	6 lb.	3 lb.	6 lb.	96 slices	3 - 6 dz.	4 lb.	2 lb.
40	7 1/2 lb.	3 3/4 lb.	7 lb.	120 slices	4 -7 dz.	5 lb.	2 1/2 lb.
48	9 lb.	4 1/2 lb.	8 lb.	144 slices	4 - 8 dz.	6 lb.	3 lb.

PERSONAL PREFERENCES

Hmmm... I like an eclectic group so I tend to not leave people out because they are odd or eccentric. Events where you can invite the odd and eccentric and have those guests stir, change, and shift the conversations away from the benign always make for a fun evening/event.

As I mentioned before, I'm a bit of social butterfly. I tend to be late a lot because I am usually having a conversation with someone in an effort to learn what I can from something they may have to offer. There was a saying in our hometown, "You're always waiting on a Kershner!"

It is this social butterfly quality that provides me with my eclectic guest lists.

That's all entertaining is really about... it's nothing more than your personal preferences, likes, dislikes, and possibly even your aspirations played out for a group of people to enjoy.

INVITATIONS

Here's what I know of invitations... the invitation should match the formality of the event. Some of the more refined etiquette teachers may disagree but this is my opinion. I'm always open for an educating lesson but I have my theories and my beliefs.

When most people think of weddings, they, or at least I do, think of the invitation in terms of fonts or scripting and wedding announcement protocols and that generally equals calligraphy. A small gathering can have invitations as well. To me, if you are going to go through the trouble of hosting an event, why not announce it with an invitation!

Since most of my events deal with family and friends, there never is a great deal of formality to my invitations. That being said, I still feel a great pull and a desire to create an invitation.

Perhaps it's just my more creative side trying to break free. I find myself fretting over the invitation for days though.

"Is this the right font?"

"Is the typeface big enough?"

"Is there to much information on the invite or not enough?"

I drive myself nuts sometimes.

At the end of the day, less is more and the invite needs to match the theme and formality of what you are envisioning and trying to pull off in terms of the event.

Now if you are trying your hand at a five-course meal, because you think it would be fun to try, those events might be a little more formal than your backyard seafood extravaganza. You might want to put a little more thought into the invitation. It's just a suggestion...

We have provided three invitation examples for you to use and build off of. Use these three invitations as samples and then play around with different fonts, font sizes, and feel free to add pictures, clip art, etc. to make the invite your own.

The first example is an invitation from when I decided to try my hand at what is considered, traditionally speaking, a French five-course meal. Here's what I had on my invitation:

Enjoy an eclectic culinary journey and join us for...

Dinner at the Kershner's

[Date here]
[Time Here]

We will be experiencing a five-course meal derived from traditional French faire and other dishes we have been waiting to sample.

We will be enjoying the following courses:

Grilled Prosciutto Wrapped Shrimp

Pan Seared Salmon with Blueberry Glaze
served on a bed of fresh steamed rice and
Grilled Sesame Asparagus

Veal Scaloppine Bolognese
with fresh steamed vegetables and red-skinned potatoes

Citrus Infused Spinach and Cranberry Salad

Cheesecake with Fresh Berry Sauce

And yes, I understand that I am a complete dork!!

The last line conveyed to the guests that while, on its face, it seemed like a formal invite and event, it was, in point-of-fact, merely the excuse or reason for the event. Me being the dork that I am, I simply wanted to try a five-course meal to see if I could do it.

Now, due to time constraints, we ditched the steamed veggies and potatoes and combined the third (Veal) and fourth (Salad) courses. This is an example of how, even though there was a "formal," or official, invite, the host, needed to work within the framework of the event. The dinner was not started on time due to a guest's late arrival.

In our second example, the invitation is to our "End of School" / "Start of Summer" party called the Low Country Boil. Every summer for the last few years, we have held this party and it serves many purposes. My wife is a high school teacher, so she is off for the summer, and the girls have finished their individual school years as well. Also, this party is usually held on, or about, the time of our anniversary. This invitation is much less formal than the 5-course meal invite.

This example also shows that you can incorporate images, drawings, or artwork of any type into your invitation. This example is a bit crude but you can get the general idea.

Your Whole Family has Been Invited to
Attend the Kershner's
4th Annual
Low Country Boil
&
Summer Kick-Off Party!

[Date Here]
[Time Here]
[Address Here]

RSVP by [Date Here]
[Phone Number Here]

For the kids, there will be a bounce house and water fun!

Bring a bathing suit and a towel!

Rain Date: [Rain Date Here]
If it rains on the [Rain Date]… see you next year!

Our third invitation example presents a Block Party invitation. Our neighborhood had some upheaval in recent years and this upheaval really served to bring neighbors, which were already friendly toward each other, even closer together. As a result, our neighborhood now hosts a yearly block party. The first year we tried the "block party" concept; we distributed the following invite via mailbox flyer or email to all of the residents on two streets:

"Problems can become opportunities when the right people come together" -Robert Redford

"Coming together is a beginning. Keeping together is progress. Working together is success." –Henry Ford

You are cordially invited to a Community Potluck / BLOCK PARTY!

[Date here]
[Time here]

Location: [Address here]

Bring your own:
Lawn Chair
Beverages
Dish to share (feeding 6-8 people)
Children: Bring bikes and scooters

We have all met so many wonderful people due to the redevelopment on our roads. We would like to take this opportunity to get to know each other outside of the city meetings and emails. This is not a meeting but a party to celebrate all of the wonderful people that live in our neighborhood.

THE CHECKLIST

The checklist is a list of things that no one really wants to do but is comprised of tasks that need to be done. Most of them are common sense type stuff and involve cleaning and putting stuff away. If you cringed at those words... you are really not going to like this list.

If you are planning on having an event, dinner, or even just a few friends for a movie night, do yourself a favor and perform the following actions:

- Clean the bathroom
- Vacuum the carpets/rugs
- Sweep the hardwoods, tile, and/or linoleum
- Address the kitchen floor
- Put away any piles of stuff
- Clean the counters/countertops
- Run the dishwasher and don't forget to empty it

You are cleaning your home to provide a certain level of comfort for your guests. I tell you these things because these are common sense items that get forgotten until the last minute... or tragically, until a guest discovers them. No matter how you slice it, or how discreetly, or politely your guest informs you, it's still embarrassing.

Outside of cleaning the actual interior, there are some things I think that need to be mentioned regarding tableware.

Check for spots on all glass and stemware, flatware, serveware, etc. If you find any, then you might want to consider a different detergent or perhaps loading your dishwasher in a different manner. Either way, take an extra 5 minutes and wash them right now with warm soapy water then towel dry them by hand... don't let them air dry or you'll be washing them again. Towel drying ensures that there will be no spots.

Collect any dishes, cups, and plates that are laying about the house and load the dishwasher... and start it. Then you actually need to empty it before you start cooking. By doing this you are enabling yourself to load it as you go with the various items used while preparing the meal. If you load as you go, you can avoid "Mt. Dishmore" at the end of the night. Clean as you go with regard to pots and pans, utensils, cutting boards, knives, etc. This is not a commercial kitchen and as such, there is no dedicated dishwasher. If you go looking for one, you'll find one in a spouse or staring back at you in the mirror.

And lastly, after everyone has gone home for the evening, clean before you go to bed. I'm not saying start over on this checklist but cleaning up prior to turning in is easier than you think. There is no better feeling than waking up the next morning and discovering the house is already clean and you can just go on with your day. Nothing is left to wash or put away, except maybe a load of dishes in the dishwasher.

PARTY PLANNING CHECKLIST

All of the items noted in "The Checklist" section technically falls within the "One Week Before" and the "1 Day Before" category of the following table. We have titled this table the "Party Planning Checklist."

In this checklist you will see items you need to either accomplish or consider the day of, the day before, or even a week or two before the event. Granted, this book is geared towards the informal gathering where the meal is, generally, a sit down meal. However, regardless of whether or not it is sit down meal or a buffet, we felt it was important to point a few of these things out.

Oddly enough, I received this in my weekly email update from our local grocery store. If your grocer has an email list you can sign up for to receive information on specials, promotions, sales, etc. it is definitely worth it.

Who wants to wait around for the Saturday or Sunday paper for the grocers circular when you can receive it a few days in advance via email?

Also, if you live in area with a larger or upscale grocery store you can place your orders, or special orders, while you do you prep/shopping for the gathering.

Party Planning Checklist

3 Weeks Before
- [ ] Make your guest list
- [ ] Plan theme and purchase decorations accordingly
- [ ] Plan menu, compile shopping list, and place any food orders

2 Weeks Before
- [ ] Clean any silverware, glass, or china, launder tablecloths Create a music playlist that will last the entire party
- [ ] Do your first round of grocery shopping for condiments and tableware

1 Week Before
- [ ] Clean up house and/or patio/yard
- [ ] Set the stage/arrange seating and designate a coffee and dessert table
- [ ] Take inventory of tableware and cookware
- [ ] Stock your bar

3 Days Before
- [ ] Notify neighbors if you expect the party to be large and parking extensive
- [ ] Decorate
- [ ] Finish grocery shopping

1 Day Before
- [ ] Set the tables or setup the buffet
- [ ] Pickup cake and prepared foods
- [ ] Buy and arrange flowers
- [ ] Do any necessary prep cooking (dicing, marinating, etc.)
- [ ] Give the house a touch up cleaning

Party Day
- [ ] Pick up ice/put canned and bottled drinks on ice
- [ ] Finish any last minute cooking
- [ ] Place chairs/setting
- [ ] Display food
- [ ] Greet guests

Snacks
- [ ] Chips
- [ ] Dips/Salsas
- [ ] Crackers
- [ ] Nuts
- [ ] Mints
- [ ] Cakes
- [ ] Cookies
- [ ] Breads

Beverages
- [ ] Soft Drinks
- [ ] Water
- [ ] Juice
- [ ] Ice
- [ ] Punch Bowl
- [ ] Pitcher
- [ ] Coffee: Regular/Decaf
- [ ] Tea: Sweet/Regular/Packets
- [ ] Creamer
- [ ] Sugar
- [ ] Beer/Wine
- [ ] Mixers

Condiments
- [ ] Ketchup
- [ ] Mustard
- [ ] Relish
- [ ] Mayonnaise
- [ ] Pickles
- [ ] Olives
- [ ] Salt/Pepper

Tableware
- [ ] Plates: Large/Small
- [ ] Forks
- [ ] Spoons
- [ ] Knives
- [ ] Cups
- [ ] Napkins
- [ ] Tablecloth
- [ ] Toothpicks

Special Touches
- [ ] Candles
- [ ] Flowers
- [ ] Camera(s)
- [ ] Gift(s)
- [ ] Seating Cards

Costs

Costs can be kept low by deriving events that defray the costs of the event among the guests. For example, when our family lived in Charlotte, we had some close friends in our neighborhood and every month we got together for something called "Supper Club."

The premise behind supper club was simple, the host provided the home and the main course, and the guests provided everything else. Essentially, it was a neighborhood potluck. At the time, my wife and I didn't have any children so we were basically assigned the month of October in order to host the Halloween party.

Never in my life have I seen so many twenty and thirty something's, respectable, professional people in their daily lives, revert to their college days with as much ease as this group of guests did. Something's are better left unsaid at this point.

WINE PAIRINGS

OK. The pairing of wine to the main course (fish, chicken, beef, etc.) can be a daunting task. Not many people are "wine connoisseurs" or sommeliers; we just know what we like. For instance, I like sweet wines so I stick mostly to Riesling and Pinot Grigio. However, we have friends that only drink red.

We have a couple of friends that will ask what is being prepared so they can bring their own bottle to drink. I am never offended by this. I would rather my guests enjoy their meal with a wine they know and like than suffer through something because the host hasn't expanded his palette to enjoy reds as much as whites. Good friends, trusted friends, can do this. And that's really the point of all of this, spending more time with family and friends.

I'm a work in progress... What can I say?

So, what do you do when the situation presents itself and you need to provide a wine in both the red and white variety?

Well, you can refer to Wine Pairing Matrix.

I found the basis for the matrix while walking through a big box store with my two girls. It was a disastrous trip, absolutely deplorable behavior by all three of us. There was a lot whining and naps were ordered for all when we returned home!

The only saving grace for the entire trip was the generalized wine pairing placard hanging above the wine racks. It was with this placard that I began to learn about wine.

The recreating of the wine-pairing table led me to mention my overall lack of understanding for wine to Scott. Scott, in turn, led me to Donny Austin. Donny Austin owns *House Wine* in Old Worthington, Ohio. Donny also teaches classes in the store for people to come in and learn about the wines so that they may better understand why they prefer certain types of wine over others.

What I wanted to understand about wines was not the pretentious details, but rather, I simply wanted to understand things about the species of grapes, the basics of notes (namely, what is a note), and some history concerning the vineyard or grower and their family.

By the way, notes are flavors in the wine derived from the soil and air.

Now, I'm still no sommelier, and I still like what I like, but now I understand certain characteristics about the wine. I now have a bit of the details and the details are what I need to connect and understand things.

WINE PAIRING MATRIX

Main Ingredient	Wine Varieties														
	Cabernet Sauvignon	Merlot	Shiraz	Pinot Noir	Zinfandel	Sangiovese (Chianti)	Champagne	Chardonnay	Sauvignon Blanc	Riesling / Gewürztraminer	Pinot Grigio	Port	Moscato	Viognier	Malbec
Beef	x	x	x	x	x	x									x
Duck	x	x	x	x	x	x									x
Chicken/Turkey		x		x	x			x		x	x			x	
Lamb	x	x	x	x	x	x									x
Chops/Shanks	x	x	x	x	x	x		x							
Game Birds	x	x	x	x	x	x		x							
Venison	x	x	x	x	x	x									x
Pork			x			x				x	x			x	x
Salmon/Tuna				x	x			x	x	x	x			x	
Tilapia/Halibut							x	x	x	x	x			x	
Shellfish			x				x	x	x	x	x			x	
Brie/Camembert	x	x		x			x		x	x	x		x	x	
Goat Cheese/ Feta					x				x	x	x		x		
Parmesan/Romano	x	x	x	x	x	x		x							x
Blue/Gorgonzola	x		x		x							x		x	
Cheddar	x	x	x		x	x		x				x		x	x
Barbecue	x		x		x										x
Asian Foods							x		x	x	x				
Pasta/White Sauce	x	x	x						x		x				
Pasta/Red Sauce			x		x	x									x

THINGS TO KNOW WHEN IT COMES TO WINE

Over the course of writing and researching the topics for this book, I asked Donnie and Scott to provide a pseudo private wine tasting. I say pseudo because the wives and girlfriends were leery of us enjoying a number of wine selections without close adult supervision. It appears they know us to well...

The reason I asked them to partake in this little adventure of mine was simple. I knew nothing about wine. As I mentioned previously, all I knew of wine was what I had seen on TV depicted by actors or read in books and I did not care for the pretentiousness in how the material was presented. I don't really care what side of the mountain it grew on or for any of the other antiquated "Lord of Manner" caste system holier-than-thou details. I only wanted to know why I liked some wines and not others.

Simple, right?

Wrong.

Before we get into what I learned, here's a little info on our "Wine Guide," Donnie Austin.

Donnie is a Certified Sommelier by the Court of Master Sommeliers. Knowing this, Scott and I have asked Donnie to assist us with the wine pairings for the menus represented in the Meal Pairing Matrix.

Just learning that he was a Certified Sommelier made me go and research the Court of Master Sommeliers to better understand their role in all of this.

I discovered that there are four levels of the sommelier, with Master Sommelier as the highest. Donnie, as a Certified Sommelier, is a Level II Sommelier.

 Basically, according to the Court website, "The Court of Master Sommeliers was established to encourage improved standards of beverage knowledge and service in hotels and restaurants." The first Master Sommelier test took place in the United Kingdom in 1969.

Did you know that there have only been 170 successful attempts at the rank of Master Sommelier in over four decades?

I was reading a local blog some time ago and the authors' husband had just attempted the Master Sommelier test and failed. Apparently, there was only one person there who passed test and she was attempting it for the 6th time. These exams are not cheap and anything over a Level II and you have to be invited to test by the Court.

Crazy.

I asked Donnie about this Master Sommelier ranking and when he might be taking the Advanced Sommelier exam. He indicated that he had been invited by the Court to sit for the exam but given the study and prep time, the cost of the exam, time away from House Wine; it was not something he was prepared to do and declined the Court's offer. When he does sit for the Advanced Exam, I wish him nothing but the best and hope he passes the first time out.

According to the Court, in order for Donnie to achieve an Advanced Sommelier ranking, he will need to, basically, survive a five day endurance challenge centered, obviously, on wine. The first step, naturally, is to be invited by the Court. From there, he must sit for three days of lectures and wine tastings which are all administered by a group of Master Sommeliers. After that, he must then take a two day exam which is broken into three parts. To summarize the three parts, Donnie would have to demonstrate an expert knowledge in the following areas:

1.) Practical restaurant wine service and salesmanship;

2.) A written theory examination based on advanced Sommelier knowledge; and finally,

3.) A blind tasting of six wines using the Deductive Tasting format.

Crazy indeed.

As you can see from all of the information noted above, it doesn't take much to get me sidetracked and researching something else instead of what I am supposed to be doing.

As I was saying, I asked Donnie and Scott to help me better understand wine by way of a private wine tasting. I also figured that I would kill two birds with one stone and use this wine tasting as a prime opportunity to try out some of the recipes Scott and I were contemplating for insertion into the book. Naturally, Scott would do the cooking.

I am exhibiting sound logic here, I assure you.

I figured that if I have a professional chef and a Certified Sommelier willing to help, why wouldn't I put that expertise to good use?

Like I said, sound logic.

During the course of the wine tasting, I learned the following about the different types of wine Donnie provided (some notes are minimal and may require more drinking, er, I mean research!):

- Alcohol content is determined by the aging process and how much time the yeast has to convert the sugars of the grape into alcohol.

- Red wines are red because of the skin of the grape not the color of the juice.

- Red wines can be chilled like a white but you need to take it out of the wine cooler with enough time for it to return to room temperature.

- Sparkling wines, like a Cava or Prosecco, complement the spiciness, saltiness, or fried nature of most appetizers.

- The most commonly known Sparkling Wine is Champagne.

- Sweet wines, like Riesling or Gewürztraminer, or even the occasional Pinot Grigio, are sweet because they don't stay in the barrel as long. As a result, there is more sugar from the fruit and some vintners add more sugar just before the bottling process.

- The general rule of thumb to determining sweetness in white wine is to observe the alcohol content noted on the bottle. If it says 11%-13% it is a dryer sweet wine but the really sweet ones are at about 8%-10.5%.

- Sauvignon Blanc should be finished off the day, or night, it is opened as it loses a great deal of flavor if the bottle must be re-corked and stored until later.

- Chardonnay can be oaky and buttery (sorry, somewhat pretentious detail there) and works well with creamy, or buttery, dishes like a Fettuccini Alfredo. This wine also works well with grilled foods.

- Pinot Noir is considered a bridge wine. A bridge is when the meal transitions from a white wine to a red wine. Most people typically pair this with a salmon dish.

- Merlot contains a lot of tannins and, as a result of that, it works best with meats that contain a lot of protein and fats.

- Tannins are when the skins of the red grapes are left in contact with the juice longer and are generally detected in a wine by that drying sensation you feel in your mouth.

- Wines high in tannins are paired with meats high in protein and fats to minimize the drying effect.

- Port is a very heavy wine that contains about 20% alcohol. Personally, I prefer cooking with it as opposed to drinking it.

- Dessert wines, like Muscat or Ice Wine, typically should be sweeter than the dessert being served.

- An Ice Wine is derived from grapes that basically become raisins on the vine, freeze on the vine, and then are pressed while frozen. This produces a nice honey flavor.

Embracing Your Inner Chef

EMBRACING YOUR INNER CHEF

"How do I do that?" is generally my first question when reading a cookbook or watching some show on TV. To solve this conundrum wrapped in a riddle, the first thing I did was look into resources available in my community.

Our suburb offers a program called "Lifelong Learning" where classes are available for everything from Seniors Water Aerobics to Languages to Painting. One of the topics they also covered was "Food and Drink." Some of the "Food" offerings were classes where students would cook five, or so, items with the assistance of a trained chef... this is where I met Scott and our friendship began.

NOTE: Some programs in your, or a neighboring, community may offer similar classes. Do some research and find out what is available in your area. Smaller communities may not offer these so check with a local college or university extension about these offerings as well. There is also a cooking implements store called Sur La Table that offers cooking classes for a fee but they are not in every city or state so check out their website for information on the store and classes nearest you.

After enrolling and attending a few classes I learned that the plush environment where we were taking classes was not always the case. I learned that prior classes were held in the cramped and antiquated Home Economics classrooms of our local high school. To hear Scott tell it, it would appear that not everything was on par with what one would expect in a restaurant or commercial style kitchen. The classes I enrolled in were, fortunately, being held at a local catering storefront.

That fall session I signed-up for two classes. I threw my culinary fate to the wind based on the following write-ups for these classes:

Tuscan Essentials

An experienced chef from this beautiful Grandview catering facility offers an evening of culinary instruction filled with fun and food. The appetizing menu features an authentic and flavorful Tuscan meal that you can recreate at home to rave reviews. The chef prepares Panzanella Salad, Homemade Ricotta Agnolotti in Sage-Infused Butter, Chicken Fricassee, and Braise Cannellini Beans with Rosemary. Learn a few Italian cooking techniques as you enjoy this informative demonstration. Sample the dishes and receive the recipes.

> ### *Très François: Fanciful French Cuisine*
>
> *Excited about his move to a great new venue, Scott, our popular former professional chef, offers an evening of French cooking made simple. Both new and returning students will enjoy this impressive yet surprisingly easy-to-prepare continental menu. In an entertaining and informative demonstration format, he wows the group with Seared Duck Breast with Fresh Berry Compote; Braised Halibut Provencal; Flat Iron Steak with Fresh Herbs; Pork and Polenta with Fontina and Parmesan Cheeses; Roasted Potatoes with Sweet Onions and Dill Soda Bread. Sample the dishes and receive the recipes.*

Everything we made in both classes was exceptional and I loved every minute of it! The important thing for me to take away from these classes was not the recipe, it was the technique applied by the chef. Everything a chef does, they do with a purpose. Everything from the manner in which something is cut and prepared to the look and smell of something as it cooks has a purpose. I've taken many classes since and I've never seen a chef use a timer. Scott has been known to get lost in conversation during these classes and is occasionally distracted by students while something is cooking in the oven. He will end up with something being a little more well-done than he would have liked but it's still good.

A chef is looking at other, or for, more specific things besides duration. They are looking for internal temperature (once it reaches the correct temperature... STOP COOKING IT!), coloring (when sautéing, brown is usually GOOD, black is usually BAD!), texture (smooth, shiny, lumpy, etc.), smell, etc.

It was in *Tuscan Essentials* that I learned that making pasta from scratch really isn't that hard. You just need some time and the right tools. I also learned that Chicken Fricassee and Pollo al Chilindron is pretty much the same thing. A professionally trained chef may argue this point but, to me, they were pretty much the same thing. The salad was very simple, as most salads are, but it was the addition of rubbing the sides of the bowl with garlic that gave the Panzanella Salad its appeal.

In the *Très François: Fanciful French Cuisine* class, I learned that wild duck and store bought duck vary considerably when it comes to fat content. Store bought duck has a ton of fat and wild duck is lean. I am no expert but I think it has everything to do with exercise.

Now, I have been duck hunting. It was not uncommon to shoot, clean, and cook the duck all in one day.

Duck is a fine meal.

However, I have *never* seen a duck, being cooked for such a short amount of time, which smoked as much as the duck we cooked that night! Now, it was delicious, just like all duck dishes that are cooked and prepared correctly, but we had the industrial sized exhaust system working overtime that night. We could barely see ten feet! Everyone had to shower and wash their clothes when they got home because the smoke and smell of that duck being cooked had permeated every pore on your body and every fiber of your clothing.

What does someone take away from that? Well, I learned that, unless I shot the duck myself, cook the thing outside! If you have a side burner on your grill, use it. When cooking store bought duck, do not ever close the lid on the grill and always cook it in a pan. Do not ever place the duck on the actual grill surface. There is too much fat in store bought duck and you are asking for a lot of flame ups and, potentially, some char grilled duck for your trouble.

Since I am an extremely inquisitive person, I also quickly discovered that there are a great many cookbooks and shows out there ready to inspire people to try something new. But I also discovered that the only thing that stops them from trying, in my estimation, is fear. Fear that they have no idea what they are referring to in a recipe, fear it will turn out poorly, fear that it will not look the same as it did on TV or in the cookbook, fear that no one will like it and on and on and on.

Times have changed. Family dynamics have changed. Society as a whole has shifted away from the agrarian aspects that came to this country hundreds of years ago and that existed prior to the Europeans arriving. Let's face it, families don't cook as much as they use to and those family recipes have ceased to be handed down. So much is being lost and I've boiled it all down to the three fears. Well, to me, there are three "fears" that people have when it comes to cooking:

1. Fear of the kitchen.

2. Fear of the recipe.

3. Fear of failure.

Since Scott is the chef, and not naturally predisposed to these fears, let's take a moment to explore these three fears and I'll explain how I overcame each.

FEAR #1 - THE KITCHEN

People have become so afraid of the stove, oven, range, cook top, appliances, etc. Items in a kitchen these days can be very intimidating, I will admit. Many people have a legitimate fear of being burned, cut, and impaled! I was able to conquer this particular fear in college. I worked as a cook in a restaurant in Boone, North Carolina called *Macado's*. It was here that I begin my culinary journey. *Macado's* served your typical college town faire with its over-stuffed sandwiches and Monday and Saturday night beer specials but the experience was invaluable. It helped me get over my fear of an oven, stove, cook top, and sharp and unusual instruments. Don't get me wrong, I still burned and cut myself, just like any beginner would, but I was able to do this in a controlled environment. This was in 1995-1996. It took a further fourteen years to cook something on my own for a group.

Remember, baby steps are still steps.

FEAR #2 - THE RECIPE

Recipes have far flung terms for ingredients, not to mention, the manner in which something is prepared. Some things just don't translate well. Ingredients, and the titles of recipes for that matter, are sometimes in a foreign language. To compound this misery, many recipes contain ingredients that are not known to the would-be chef. Ingredients like "radicchio" for example.

Fortunately, anyone can conquer this fear with minimal amounts of research in the written word or on the Internet. Ingredients and terminology can be deciphered with the help of cookbooks that offer greater descriptions of terms, styles, and techniques as well. The Internet is also a valuable resource. There are numerous options out there so there is no excuse for not knowing nowadays. *YouTube* is a very valuable resource for visual demonstrations if you are unsure of something that has been written.

By the way, a radicchio, at least, according to Wikipedia, is:

> *"...a leaf chicory (Cichorium intybus, Asteraceae), sometimes known as Italian chicory. It is grown as a leaf vegetable which usually has white-veined red leaves. It has a bitter and spicy taste, which mellows when it is grilled or roasted."* I looked it up.

To me, it looks like a red cabbage but apparently it is not the same so don't be confused by its appearance.

Fear #3 - Fear of Failure

All of the "what if's" and the range of emotions that a writer or artist producing and displaying their work typically ebbs and flows through runs through the synapses of a would-be chef as well. Sometimes it is enough to stop them from trying new textures, flavors, techniques, or recipes entirely. Just because something is new or different doesn't mean that it isn't worth trying. It's only then that you can make a fair assertion of whether or not you actually like or dislike something.

Implementing a back-up plan conquered this fear for me. It helps to have a back-up plan in case things go horribly wrong. My back-up plan contains two easily attainable parts.

Part 1 of the back-up plan is to laugh. If something doesn't work and induces quizzical looks, or looks of bewilderment and horror, then all you have really done is create a memorable experience. Sometimes those are the funniest stories to re-tell. It is just food. Which, I know, is a very overindulgent American thing to say, but in this case it's true.

Part 2 of the back-up plan is to have something at the ready in case it needs to be called upon. In our house, if we try something new and it stinks, for whatever reason, we throw it out and order a pizza. No fear.

We have a back-up plan, the pizza. We even tell guests at dinner parties we host, "We are trying something new so be prepared for this or pizza."

Fortunately, we have never had to revert to the back-up pizza when guests were present. However, I have ruined my fair share of meals and desserts when they weren't present. Here are two quick little stories for you to laugh at me about.

Shortly after we were married, I called my dad for his meatloaf recipe. The reason for this is two-fold. One, I liked it because it incorporated hard-boiled eggs inside it and two, my wife had recently made her mother's meatloaf and I was not a fan.

As I was on the phone with my father, I very studiously wrote down every word but I think "Ma Bell" was having issues with her phone lines that day because I missed the one key word that ruined the meal forever.

That word was "or."

His recipe called for a pack of onion soup mix OR a certain amount of salt. I incorrectly transcribed the word "and" for "or."

Now, I don't know if you have ever used an onion soup packet but there is a LOT of sodium in those things. Take that and couple it with amount of salt it called for and you have yourself a bonafide salt lick suitable only for livestock!

Domino's anyone?

As if that wasn't bad enough, here's another one...

Have you ever had a craving for something specific but then you make it and its ruined forever?

Well I have.

A few years back, I became enamored with the iced lemon poppy seed cake slices available at *Caribou Coffee*. So I set my sights to making my own cake. Now, I do need to point out that I am not baker nor have I ever claimed to be. Anyway, I dedicated myself to finding this cake recipe online. By the way, I know I have mentioned numerous online resources but don't believe everything you read online... this next part is why not.

So I made the lemon poppy seed cake and followed the directions to the letter. Whenever I make something for the first time I follow the recipe exactly. It is only after I have tasted the finished product do I make it my own by amending the ingredients list and quantity amounts.

So I followed the recipe and just like the recipe stated, it had the most perfect crust. Just like it was supposed to. Unfortunately, the inside of the cake had the consistency, and texture, of beach sand!

I sent the recipe to a friend, who happens to be a Pastry Chef, and she remarked that putting six eggs and vast quantities of powdered sugar in a cake recipe is apparently *never* a good idea.

She wasn't surprised the cake turned out the way it did.

I'll say it again; I'm not a baker.

How was I supposed to know that?

It was at this point that Scott educated me on the difference between "mechanical" and "natural" cooks. We will talk about this concept in a little bit.

As I look back, and this falls into the "no fear" and "why not" motif I am associating with cooking, I can honestly say the reason I have no fear of cooking is, in large part, due to my wife, Tricia.

Shortly after we were married, I was afforded the opportunity to go to Europe for business and Tricia came with me. We made the classic rookie American abroad mistake; we sought comfort food in the form of American chain restaurants instead of embracing what the region had to offer. We only made that mistake once and fortunately for us, this occurred on the first day.

Much like the Montezuma's Revenge legend of drinking the water in Latin America, Americanized chain restaurants in Europe do not use the same ingredients, prepare the food, or cook the food the same as in the States and thusly, gut wrenching pain ensued.

It was at this point we decided to "go native." We didn't look at a menu; we didn't order "off menu" or ask for something to be prepared a certain way. We didn't ask for ingredients to be substituted or left out. No. We simply ordered the café, bistro, or restaurant specialty, what the server recommended as their favorite, or the special of the day. However they were selling it, we were eating it. And it didn't disappoint! (Granted, we do not have any dietary restrictions so this may not work for everyone.)

It was from this experience that I got over my irrational fear of unknown foods and to stop being so picky and try new things. That is, except for fresh cheese. I don't know what it is about cheese but the only thing I can equate it to would be like giving a dog peanut butter. That's what I look like with a mouth full of cheese. It's not pretty and I try to avoid it.

Now, I have mentioned several broad topics: catering, hosting, and cooking. What I have not explained to you is that all three are inter-connected. Catering and hosting are about presentation and providing a relaxing and enjoyable experience for your guests. Cooking is about the preparation and presentation of a meal. However, your outdoor space plays an important role as well. Gardening, for that matter, is about the presentation and cultivation of your outdoor space. Presentation of the garden, flowerbeds, the yard as a whole, can inspire themes and colors and promote a relaxing atmosphere. Items grown in the garden can be harvested to complement the dish you are preparing for the event.

Did you know that the single most expensive ingredients in any dish, by weight, are the herbs and spices?

These items can be grown and maintained in your own garden for the cost of a pack of seed and some water. If you have a tendency to use a particular herb in many meals, you should consider growing and maintaining that item in your garden or home year round. An herb box or pot grown in the windowsill will offer a new fragrance into your home during the winter months. It will also provide greenery as a relaxing reminder of warmer days.

Everything you do and don't do when entertaining is a reflection of you and your personality. Your likes and dislikes, your tastes... basically, all of your preferences in life will be reflected in the manner in which you host an event.

MECHANICAL VS. NATURAL

As I took more classes, I learned more about the instructor's individual backgrounds and the, sometimes, colorful paths to the kitchen. Most had formal Culinary School training and then went on to pay their dues as line cooks and worked their way up to Rounds Cook, Shift Chef (day or night), Sous Chef, Working Chef, Chef, and on to Executive Chef.

But after talking, watching, and learning from Scott, I learned that there are two types of cooks. There are mechanical cooks and natural cooks.

A mechanical cook follows the recipe to the letter. A 1/4 t means a 1/4 t and ten minutes means ten minutes. Mechanical cooks make great bakers. They also make great cooks in resorts where there are multiple restaurants that need to repeat the same exact recipe regardless of the restaurant they are assigned to. They may take a little longer to perfect a recipe, but once they get it, they have it forever without variation.

A natural cook reads the recipe and creates it pretty close to the original the first time. They ascertain the general idea of the recipe and then re-create the dish with approximate measurements, durations, and often substitute ingredients for whatever is nearby, handy, plentiful, or suits their personal taste. The results are the same, more or less, but the natural cook understands the "goal state." This can sometimes be dangerous to their guests if the chef likes bold flavors. Bold flavors may be a bit of spice, heat, or odd combinations that could be too much for their guest's palate.

Think back to your math classes in grammar school. Was there a student that was repeatedly harangued by the instructor to show their work and yet the answer was correct?

It's the same for a natural cook. They'll get the answer right but are oftentimes unable to tell you what they did to get to the end result.

FRESH VS. PROCESSED

I've taken many cooking classes/demonstrations and it didn't matter whom the chef (instructor) was, each was equally hell bent on railing against processed foods.

I have read a great deal of information regarding the debate between fresh vs. processed foods in various books, articles, magazines, websites, promotional material, as well as, movie documentary, Internet group and blog material. Each had their own slant, be it political or other, but they were all consistent in their support of local growers, growers that employ organic growing techniques, growers that avoid pesticides, frequenting local/community farmer's markets, farmers that raise their livestock humanely without hormones, etc.

I highly recommend the documentaries *Food, Inc.*, *Food Matters*, and *Vanishing of the Bees*, as well as, the book titled *Skinny Bitch*. These resources will open your eyes to a great many things.

Without getting out the soapbox, and being overly preachy, I tell you that there is a noticeable difference between dishes made with natural ingredients and dishes made with processed ingredients. Natural ingredients taste better, setup better, and are overall better for you. Not to mention, supporting your local growers and farmers is good for your local economy as well. This year, and in the years following, I look forward to donating my extra produce for distribution to a local food pantry. Food Pantry's are always looking for fresh vegetables to provide to those in need.

As an example, I was reading an article in our local paper, May 10, 2010 – *Columbus Dispatch*, titled "Tater Tots? I Think Not" written by a local columnist named Jennifer Smith Richards. Apparently, a small local school district ended its contract with a larger neighboring school district and started a new contract with a vending company that "focuses of fresh, local ingredients and on-site cooking." A business manager for the company was quoted in the article as saying, "corn syrup, processed, hormones, pesticides - those are all dirty words here."

I say, "Good for them."

Fresh cooking, fresh ingredients, and foods low in trans fats are very high on the nation's social conscience right now. The article brings a lot of the issues associated with processed foods to the forefront; chief among them is the belief that fresh ingredients cost too much. The article mentioned that by going to fresh ingredients, the school district added $0.10 to the lunch prices for the coming school year.

10 cents!

That's it?

Amazing!

Go fresh. You won't regret it... It may mean a few minutes of extra prep time to grate your own cheese, or to create your own homemade stocks but, in the end, it's worth it.

Here's something to ponder as you decide which side of the fence you are on.

Cheese. When you grate a block of cheese in your home, does it stick together? "Umm, why yes, it sure does Dave, why do you ask?" OK. Stick with me here... Does the pre-grated prepackaged cheese ever stick together? "Well... no. No it doesn't. Why is that Dave?"

I'll tell you why. It is because they have included an anti-caking agent into the processing and packaging of the cheese.

If you make two of the exact same dish, one has fresh grated cheese, and the other contains pre-grated packaged cheese, I swear to you, you can taste a difference. Sauces containing fresh grated cheese will be rich and creamy and shimmer with a silky finish. The sauces containing pre-grated packaged cheese will be noticeably more bland and contain granular lumps. By the way, the lumps are the caking agent.

Did you know that one of the first items of focus a chef contemplates when deciding to open a restaurant is, "where can I get the fruits and the vegetables?" "Are the vegetables local or thousands of miles away?" The ability to ask a farmer about his growing practices goes a long way to determining the menu, seasonal ingredient possibilities, etc.

Why does the chef want to know this?

Well, if you had a choice between an ingredient grown 30 miles away and ripened on the vine versus one that was grown thousands of miles away and ripened somewhere on the journey, which one would you prefer? That's not really a choice is it? This decision can determine if the restaurant is successful or not.

In another article in the *Columbus Dispatch*, dated June 14, 2011, the Restaurant Writer, Denise Trowbridge, wrote about a local restaurant named *Latitude 41* that had recently started a garden ingeniously placed on the roof of the hotel where the restaurant is located.

According to the article, "The fruits of that 80-square-foot plot will be used in the food that MacLennan and his staff serve at Latitude 41, known for eclectic fare using seasonal, local ingredients." Chef Dave MacLennan and his staff have planted a wide assortment of vegetables and herbs with the aid of a local seed manufacturer named Wayward Seed Farm from nearby Marysville, Ohio. The garden itself was made with recycled products and donated dirt and incorporates rain barrels for their watering needs via drip irrigation.

Ms. Trowbridge wrote that, "The herbs are the key." Chef MacLennan went on to say that, "They are very expensive to buy, but we think they're going to flourish in our garden. They'll grow rapidly, and we'll be able to keep harvesting them throughout the season."

This article only further supports my previous statement that herbs and spices are the single most expensive ingredient.

If you have a proclivity toward natural ingredients, I also suggest you look into *Slow Food U.S.A.* which is an organization that aims to promote healthier eating and agricultural endeavors throughout the country.

Interesting Factoid: Did you know that there is a disease that is almost an entirely American disease that, some, in the medical community believe to be derived from eating too much processed food? It is called diverticulitis. People with this particular disease are generally instructed to alter their diet to a low residue diet. This means less processed foods and an increase in the incorporation of fresher ingredients. Watch "Food Matters" for more on this subject.

Columbus also affords many of its residents with the opportunity to

 purchase "fresh" ingredients by way of various markets. Many of my IT assignments have me working in both the suburbs and downtown Columbus. When downtown, I like to wander through the

North Market and the open-air Pearl Street Alley Farmer's Market. Our suburb also offers an open-air farmer's market on Wednesday's from May to October.

What's great about these farmer's markets is that you get the opportunity to speak with the grower about their farm, their fertilizing techniques, and growing practices. Some farmers also offer Community

Supported Agriculture (CSA). The premise behind this is the support of locally grown, mostly organic, growers. You purchase a share and the farmer makes bulk deliveries for a community to a local farmer's market weekly where you pick up your week's worth of fresh vegetables. Everyone wins! The family buys and supports local business and farming and they receive fresh ingredients in return.

I have so much more on this topic but I think I'll reserve that for a later Volume.

KNIFE SKILLS

Have you ever noticed that experienced chefs rarely, if ever, cut themselves?

Why is that?

I attended a "Knife Skills" class to ascertain why this is the case. However, before you start picturing images of "West Side Story," I need to explain that the class was focused on proper knife techniques in the kitchen. The class was taught by Scott but was not part of the typical community based Lifelong Learning courses I normally take.

Here's what I discovered after taking the class... a chef, or any professional for that matter, rarely cuts themselves because of the manner, or shape, in which they form their non-cutting hand when holding the item. A professional forms their non-cutting hand into the shape of a "C" with the tips of the fingers bent back toward the palm and out of the way of the blade.

They use the flat part of the bent fingers, between your first and second knuckle, to guide the knife to cut where you want it to cut. The

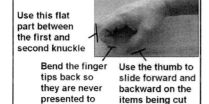

Use this flat part between the first and second knuckle

Bend the finger tips back so they are never presented to the knife

Use the thumb to slide forward and backward on the items being cut

side of the knife will rest against the finger. Most of you will be wary of the feel of the blade against your fingers. However, Scott did point out something worth noting during class. What has

more invested in the process of cutting with a sharp knife, your eyes or your fingers? Your eyes will let you down but if your fingers are telling the blade where to go, there is a far less likelihood of them getting cut by the blade.

Professionals also reduce the likelihood of cutting themselves by cutting a flat spot on items that are prone to roll. These could be items like potatoes and carrots. By cutting in a flat spot, it provides a solid foundation for cutting, slicing, dicing, etc.

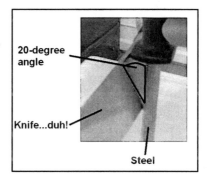

20-degree angle

Knife...duh!

Steel

Another item of note from the Knife Skills class was the correct manner in which to hone the knife. Believe it or not, there is a difference between honing and sharpening. A knife is sharpened with a grinder or a sharpening stone (also called a water stone or a whetstone). The knife should be honed on the "steel" every time you pull it from the drawer. The steel is that 12"-16" long piece of sword looking material attached to a handle that knocks about in your junk drawer with all of the other kitchen implements... like the garlic press, the peeler, and the zester.

To use the steel, as a beginner, hold the steel vertically, with the tip on the counter, and place the cutting edge of the knife at a 20-degree angle to the steel. In one fluid motion, gently slide the length of the blade against the steel as you move the blade from top to bottom. (Once you reach the bottom, don't bang the blade on the counter top!) Repeat the process with the blade on the other side of the steel so you can hone the other side of the knife.

Repeat this process 2-3 times and the knife is now honed and ready for use.

TOOLS & IMPLEMENTS

It is important to understand that tools and implements used in entertaining do not have to be top of the line or carry a specific name brand. The only thing that they have to be is functional. However, there are a few caveats to this statement.

For example, if you need to sear something and the recipe calls for you to deglaze the pan with wine; you might not want to use your non-stick pan as it contains a surface that would prohibit this technique. Chances are, if you need to deglaze the pan, the recipe is most likely going to use that seared material for gravy, or sauce, or something else further on in the recipe. This is why it is vitally important that you read through the entire recipe before you start cooking it. In the same vein, if you are using your non-stick pans, do not use a metal implement to stir or flip anything in the pan as it may scratch the non-stick surface.

My point here is, just because you've decided you want to be a better cook, or start entertaining more, you don't need to go out and replace everything in your kitchen.

If you can justify the purchase of a particular item, then by all means go get one. But if you can't think of but one or two recipes that may call for that tool or implement, then you can probably make do using something else. I am in this quandary now...

I would like to obtain the tools necessary to make homemade pasta. But the nagging thought in the back of my brain is saying, "You are going to make homemade pasta once or twice and be done with it." Therefore, I don't own any pasta making equipment right now. That is, until I decide I want to start making more dishes from scratch where I'll need those tools more often.

All you really need to get started is a couple of good pots and pans (with lids), some measuring cups and spoons, some mixing bowls, and some bake ware. As you become more proficient in the kitchen, you can simply add things as you go or as you need them more frequently. Of course the national retail stores carry about every utensil, pot, or pan you will ever need. That being said, Scott has interjected that smaller, regional, or family owned retail shops could sometimes be more economical. Other places where you can pick up that one pan or odd pot or appliance to complement your kitchen includes box stores, grocery stores, and smaller mom and pop appliance stores. Items in these places can be as little as half the price of the better-known specialty stores.

THE PANTRY LIST

You may be asking yourself, "What's a Pantry List?"

Well, a pantry list is a list of basic items each kitchen should have, at a minimum, in order to prepare food on a regular basis. The following pantry lists are broken into "Baking" and "Chef" for a reason. Most cooks tend to have a specialty, either baking of cooking. As a result of this, we have provided two fairly extensive lists as a guide. Please, please, please, consider these lists as a guides and not gospel. You don't need to run out and drop a couple hundred dollars for all of these items. Acquire these items over time until they become staples in your home. You may not need all of this stuff depending on dietary restrictions, family size, preferences, etc.

BAKER'S PANTRY LIST

Refrigerator		
Must Have		
Eggs	Milk / Cream / Half & Half	Butter (unsalted)
Nice to Have		
Cream cheese	Buttermilk (dry buttermilk powder in the baking aisle-keep in fridge)	Puff Pastry and/or Phyllo dough

Produce		
Must Have		
n/a		
Nice to Have		
Lemons	Limes	Oranges

Dry Goods		
Must Have		
Baking Powder	Brown Sugar	Chocolate chips
Baking Soda	Cocoa	Flour
Nuts	Powdered Sugar	Raisins
Sugar	Unsweetened choc squares (like a box of Bakers - keeps a long time)	
Nice to Have		
Cake Flour	Cream of Tartar (stabilize egg whites)	Dried fruits
Graham crackers	Instant espresso/coffee (for mocha)	Jimmies (chocolate/multi-color sprinkles)
Coconut Flakes	Cookies (for crumbling)	Vanilla beans
Yeast		

Canned / Bottled		
Must Have		
Food colors	Vanilla Extract	
Nice to Have		
Apricot or Apple jelly (melt to glaze desserts)	Evaporated and sweetened condensed milk (these are NOT interchangeable)	Honey
Maraschino cherries	Molasses	Extracts (ex. Almond)
Paste food color-better color-less liquid, lasts a long time	Clear corn syrup	

Vinegar / Oil		
Must Have		
Baking spray	Crisco-solid (biscuits, pie crust)	Oil-canola or other mild/unflavored liquid oil
Nice to Have		
n/a		

Wine / Spirits		
Must Have		
n/a		
Nice to Have		
Liquors (for flavoring)		

Spices		
Must Have		
Cinnamon	Salt	
Nice to Have		
n/a		

Equipment		
Must Have		
8" round cake pans	Hand Mixer	Rolling pin
9 x 13 pan	Loaf pan	Rubber spatulas
Baking liners (cupcake cups)	Measuring spoons and Cups	Straight edge spatula (for frosting)
Mixing bowls	Muffin tins-recommend non-stick	Whisk
Pie tin/pan	Wire cooling racks	
Nice To Have		
Birthday candles	Kitchen Aid or other nice stand mixer	Parchment paper
Bread knife	Zester	Pastry bags and tips
Bundt cake pan	Cardboard cake circles	Pastry brushes
Candy thermometer	Turntable (for frosting)	

CHEF'S PANTRY LIST

Refrigerator		
Must Have		
Eggs	Ripe olives	Parmesan cheese
Butter or margarine	Assorted pickles	Romano cheese
Milk	Salsa	Green olives
Bacon (freeze before "use by" date)	Jellies or jams	Mayonnaise
Horseradish	Mild cheese	Yellow mustard
Ketchup	Sharp cheese	Dijon mustard
Pickle Relish	Mozzarella	
Nice to Have		
Whipping cream	Hot pepper pickles	Apple butter
Sour cream	Worcestershire sauce	Refrigerator biscuits
Cream cheese	Steak sauce	Pancetta (freeze before "use by" date)

Freezer		
Must Have		
Ice	Boneless pork chops	Beef Stock
Vegetables	Link and/or bulk sausage	Boneless chicken breasts
Ground beef	Bacon	Chicken stock
Nice to Have		
Non-dairy topping	Prebaked pizza shells	Ground turkey or chicken
Walnuts	Flour tortillas	Whole chicken
Pecans	Corn tortillas	Fresh breadcrumbs
Almonds	Hors d'ouevres (pre-made)	Fish stock
Breads and rolls		

Produce		
Must Have		
White potatoes	Tomatoes	Garlic
Onions	Celery Apples	Carrots
Nice to Have		
Sweet potatoes	Cucumbers	Sweet peppers
Fresh mushrooms	Oranges	Hot peppers
Dried mushrooms	Lemons	Fresh herbs
Lettuce	Limes	Bananas

Dry Goods		
Must Have		
All-purpose flour	Pasta, white and/or whole grain (such as):	Wild rice
Granulated sugar	Penne or ziti	Kidney beans
Brown sugar	Spaghetti	White beans
Baking soda	Angel hair	Black beans
Baking powder	Fettuccini	Lentils
Yeast (Freeze for longer shelf life)	Linguini	Crackers
Long grain rice	Lasagna	Dried breadcrumbs
Brown rice		
Nice to Have		
Pasta, white and/or whole grain (such as):	Cornstarch	Cereal
Ditalini	Unsweetened cocoa	Basmati Rice
Orzo	Unsweetened chocolate	Couscous
Elbows Egg noodles	Semi or bitter sweet chocolate	Chick peas
Whole wheat flour	Biscuit mix	Split peas
Cornmeal	Oatmeal	Dried corn
Confectioner's sugar		

Canned/Bottled		
Must Have		
Whole tomatoes	Barbecue Sauce	Peanut butter
Tomato paste	Dijon mustard	Jams or jellies
Tomato sauce	Green beans	Assorted pickles
Crushed tomatoes	Whole kernel corn	Olives
Chicken broth	Kidney beans	Honey
Beef broth	Black beans	Hot sauce
Vegetable broth	White or pink beans	
Nice to Have		
Condensed cream of mushroom soup	Hoisin sauce	Canned chilies
Canned fruits	Salsa (extra)	Light or dark corn syrup
Pie fillings	Taco sauce	Pure maple syrup
Worcestershire sauce	Evaporated milk	Pure vanilla
Soy sauce	Sweetened condensed milk	Almond flavoring

Vinegar / Oil		
Must Have		
Olive oil	Cooking oil spray	White wine vinegar
Extra-Virgin olive oil	Red wine vinegar	White distilled vinegar
Canola oil	Balsamic vinegar	Apple cider vinegar
Nice to Have		
Peanut oil	Olive oil spray	Sesame oil

Wine / Spirits		
Must Have		
Dry red wine	Dry white wine	Dry sherry
Nice to Have		
Port Wine	Gin	Dark beer
Dry Vermouth	Rum	Light beer
Brandy or Cognac	Fruit liqueurs	

Dried Herbs		
Must Have		
Parsley	Rosemary	Bay leaves
Oregano	Thyme	Dill weed
Basil		
Nice to Have		
Rubbed sage	Savory	Chopped onions
Marjoram	Tarragon	Garlic powder
Cilantro	Dill seed	Minced garlic
Chives	Onion powder	

Spices		
Must Have		
Black peppercorns (whole)	Coarse salt	Sea Salt
Pepper	Table salt	Kosher Salt
Nice to Have		
Green Peppercorn	Ground allspice	Caraway seeds
Cinnamon sticks	Ground mace	Fennel seeds
Ground cinnamon	Pickling spice	Ground ginger
Ground nutmeg	Mustard seeds	Ground cumin
Whole nutmeg	Ground mustard	Ground Chili peppers
Ground cloves	Cayenne pepper	Red Chili flakes
Whole cloves	Celery seed	Ground sweet paprika
Ground turmeric		

COOKING PRIMER

Before we dive into some recipes to help you on your journey, I thought I'd include some helpful cooking guides. The diagrams, and the related descriptions, are generally available online and in various books. I enjoy doing research but I understand that many folks do not so I took the guesswork out of it for you.

BEEF

Beef is, by far, the more popular and most prevalent ingredient when you think of cookouts, stews, etc. That being said, the best thing I ever did for myself, in terms of cooking, was to learn how to cook a good piece of beef in a variety of ways. But in order to do that, I had to understand the characteristics of the meat I was purchasing. Hopefully this will aid you in your quest.

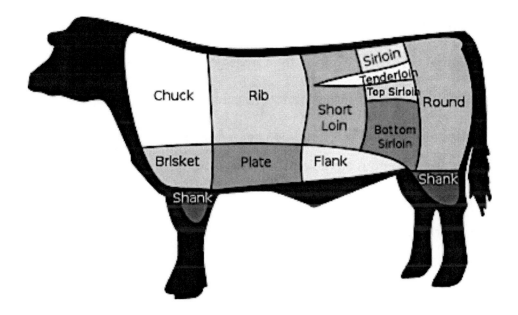

As any butcher worth their salt will tell you, beef is divided into primal cuts. Primals, as they are referred to, are further broken down into individual steaks and other cuts. A "side" of beef is literally one side of the beef carcass that is split through the backbone. Each of the sides is then halved between the 12th and 13th ribs. These two halves of the "side" are called the forequarter and hindquarter. The most-tender cuts of beef, like the rib and tenderloin, are the ones furthest from the horn and the hoof. Neck and leg muscles are worked the most, obviously, which makes them tougher. However, before we get to the cuts of beef, here are some handy definitions to help you understand certain cooking techniques. These techniques are used for both beef and pork:

Definitions:

Braising: Sear the exterior, then transition to dry or moist heat

Dry-Heat Cooking: Roasting, low to medium heat

Moist Heat: Sear and stew – long duration low to medium temp with liquids and numerous ingredients

Now that that's out of the way, let's start with the forequarter and then work our way around.

Beef Cuts – Forequarter:

Chuck: Contains parts from the neck, shoulder blade, and the upper portions of the legs. Chuck is tough with a good deal of connective tissue. This cut of meat is good for braising and stewing, particularly in a pot roast. Also, because of its fat content, chuck is good for making ground beef.

Rib: Specifically the center section of rib. Rib is used for the traditional standing rib roast (e.g. prime rib). Due to its tenderness, it is good for dry-heat cooking.

Brisket: A tough cut similar to chuck but frequently used for pot roast. Generally used for making corned beef.

Plate: Also called the short plate, it includes short ribs and skirt steak. Skirt Steak is used for making carne asada. It too contains a lot of cartilage, which makes it good for braising and can also used for making ground beef.

Shank: The shank is the leg of the animal and each side contains two shanks (one in the forequarter and one in the hindquarter.) It is extremely tough and full of connective tissue. Shank is typically used when making Osso Buco.

Beef Cuts – Hindquarter:

Short Loin: Contains many of the most desirable cuts of meat – T-bone steaks, Porterhouse steaks, Strip steak. Dry-heat cooking is best for these mostly tender cuts.

Sirloin: Still a tender cut and good for roasting or barbecuing.

Tenderloin: The finest cut of beef and it is found inside the loin. This is where the Filet Mignon comes from (the tip of the pointy end of the tenderloin). Tenderloin should only be cooked using dry heat methods such as grilling and broiling.

Flank: If not marinated first, the flank can be tough when grilled. It is better suited for braising or for making ground beef.

Round: Is a lean, but tough, cut. You are better off preparing this cut using moist-heat, as in a Crockpot.

PORK

Here's the thing about pork... several years ago, my family and I were treated to a trip to Sedona, Arizona by my in-laws. We highly recommend the *Pink Jeeps Tours* and *Off-Road Adventures* while visiting Sedona by the way... Anyway, while in Arizona, we journeyed to the Grand Canyon and had the most divine pork we have ever tasted at the *El Tovar Hotel*. It was so juicy I was scared to death I would get trichinosis! However, after a little research, and a nice and engaging discussion with the Head Chef at *El Tovar*, I discovered that once it reaches 140 - 145-degrees, stop cooking it and let it rest. If you do this, you will have a nice and juicy, but fully cooked, piece of pork. If you want to suck all of the moisture out of it, like mom or grandma used to do, then by all means cook it to 160-degrees where it is considered well done.

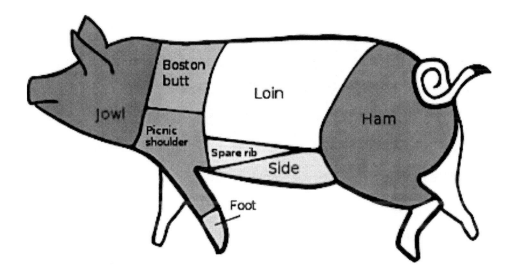

The butcher should also be able to tell you that pork is very similar to beef in that it is divided into large sections called primal cuts. The primals are then broken down into individual cuts. However, unlike beef, pork is not split into sides. Instead, it is broken down directly into its main cuts. The tenderest cuts of pork are from the rib and loin, just like with beef. It's where we get the expression "high on the hog" — the most desirable cuts of meat come from higher up on the animal. And, as with beef, the shank and shoulder muscles give us the toughest cuts due to the frequency of use by the animal.

Pork Cuts:

Boston Butt: This name is a bit of a misnomer because the Boston Butt comes from the upper shoulder of the hog. The Boston Butt is similar to chuck on a side of beef as it contains parts of the neck, shoulder blade, and upper leg. This cut is somewhat tough and contains a good deal of connective tissue. Boston Butt can be roasted or cut into steaks, but does well when braised or stewed or ground for sausages. Just above this cut is a section of fat called the clear plate or fatback. This fat is used in making lard, salt pork, and can be added to sausage or ground pork.

Picnic Shoulder: This cut is also tough because it contains part of the leg. The Picnic Shoulder is frequently cured or smoked and can even be roasted, but it's not really ideal for roasting. This cut is good for ground pork or sausage meat.

Loin: Hogs are bred to have extra long loins. They can have up to 17 ribs whereas beef and lamb only have 13. The entire pork loin can be roasted, or it can be cut into individual chops or cutlets. The tenderloin piece of the loin is taken from the rear of the loin and baby-back ribs come from the upper ribcage area of the loin. Just like Boston Butt, the loin contains another section of fatback that can be used for making lard, salt pork, or added to sausage or ground pork.

Ham: The back leg of the hog is where we get the traditional fresh, smoked, or cured hams. Serrano ham and Prosciutto are made from hams that are cured, smoked, and then air-dried. Fresh hams are usually roasted, but they can be cut into steaks as well.

Side or Belly: The side or belly cut is where we get pancetta and bacon. Belly meat can be rolled and roasted or cut into steaks as well.

Spareribs: Often prepared by grilling very slowly over low temperatures, this cut is taken from the belly side of the ribs where they join the breastbone. Spareribs can also be braised or cooked in a crock pot.

Jowl / Ham Hock: The jowl and the ham hock provide a natural smoky flavor when added to stocks and soups.

Foot: The feet of the hog are high in collagen and are the source of gelatin used in soups and stews. To tenderize this cut, you need to slowly simmer for a long period of time to break down the tough connective tissue. The foot can also be cured, smoked, or even pickled. Pig feet are a key ingredient in the traditional Mexican dish called Menudo.

Internal Temperatures

Now that you have some understanding of the characteristics of what you are purchasing, regardless of how you chose to cook it, here are the internal temperatures you must achieve to reach your desired level of doneness:

BEEF, LAMB, AND POULTRY

Roasts, Steaks & Chops		
Appearance / Cooking Style	Temperature	Description & Comments
Rare	120 to 125-degrees	Center is bright red, pinkish toward the exterior portion
Medium Rare	130 to 135-degrees	Center is very pink, slightly brown toward the exterior portion
Medium	140 to 145-degrees	Center is light pink, outer portion is brown
Medium Well	150 to 155-degrees	Not pink
Well Done	160-degrees and up	Uniformly brown throughout
Ground Meat	160 to 165-degrees	No longer pink but uniformly brown throughout
Poultry		
Type	Temperature	Description & Comments
Chicken & Duck	165-degrees	Cook until juices run clear
Turkey	165-degrees	Juices run clear - leg moves easily
NOTE: A 12-lb turkey can easily rest for 60-90 minutes, and during that time, the internal temperature can raise 20-degrees.		
Stuffing	165-degrees	Cooked alone or in turkey

PORK

Roasts, Steaks & Chops		
Appearance / Cooking Style	Temperature	Description & Comments
Medium	140 to 145-degrees	Pale pink center
Well Done	160-degrees and up	Steak is uniformly brown throughout
Pork Ribs & Shoulders		
Appearance / Cooking Style	Temperature	Description & Comments
Medium to Well Done	160-degrees and up	The longer and slower you cook, the better
Sausage (raw)	160-degrees	No longer pink
Ham		
Purchased State	Temperature	Description & Comments
Raw	160-degrees	Raw ham must be cooked thoroughly but not devoid of moisture
Pre-cooked	140-degrees	A pre-cooked Ham only needs to be re-heated

SEAFOOD

Fish (steaks, filleted, or whole)		
Appearance / Cooking Style	*Temperature*	*Description & Comments*
	140-degrees	Flesh is opaque, flakes easily
Tuna, Swordfish, & Marlin		
Appearance / Cooking Style	*Temperature*	*Description & Comments*
Medium-Rare	125-degrees	For Sword Fish and Marlin, cook to medium-rare. Tuna should cook to rare, but do not cook past medium-rare
Shrimp		
Appearance / Cooking Style	*Time*	*Description & Comments*
Medium-size, boiling	3 to 4 minutes	No more than medium rare
Large-size, boiling	5 to 7 minutes	
Jumbo-size, boiling	7 to 8 minutes	
Any Size, grilling	2-3 minutes per side	
Lobster		
Appearance / Cooking Style	*Time*	*Description & Comments*
Boiled, whole - 1 lb.	12 to 15 minutes	Meat turns red and opaque in center when cut
Broiled, whole - 1 1/2 lbs.	3 to 4 minutes	
Steamed, whole - 1 1/2 lbs.	15 to 20 minutes	
Baked, tails - each	15 minutes	
Broiled, tails - each	9 to 10 minutes	

Scallops		
Appearance / Cooking Style	*Time*	*Description & Comments*
Bake	12 to 15 minutes	Milky white or opaque, and firm
Broil		
Sear	Very high heat in oil or drawn butter 2 to 3 minutes per side	Caramelized appearance
Clams, Mussels, Oysters		
Appearance / Cooking Style	*Time*	*Description & Comments*
Steamed		Point at which their shells open - throw away any that do not open

Meal Pairing Matrix

MEAL PAIRING MATRIX

OK. Now that we have talked about the three parts that make up entertaining and all of the details associated with each, it's now time to talk food. Before we get into the recipes, we think it is important to discuss the Meal Pairing Matrix and how it works.

The Meal Pairing Matrix contains a sample menu on each row. Each menu row contains, potentially, five dishes and a beverage (beer or wine). If you don't drink, or have allergy considerations, then by all means, make substitutions. The matrix has been provided as a guide to get you started in entertaining small gatherings.

You will notice very quickly that both Scott and I have many tastes and influences. These tastes are readily shown in the countries, regions, and cultures represented in the twelve menus. You will find menus inspired by the French, Italians, and Spanish, as well as, the seasons, and regions of the United States.

Each menu contains dishes that complement one another either through consistent ingredients, spices, flavors, or textures. The sample menus also contain dishes whose recipes consist of varying degrees of difficulty. There is a great deal of variety to choose from regarding the reason for the event. As such, we have tried to provide recipes that are equal parts indoor and outdoor so you have some options depending on the season, weather, or event type. Our friend, Donnie, has provided the beverage selections noted in the matrix. He has chosen to stay within the six main, or primary, varietals of wine for *Volume I* in an effort to keep it simple. Future Volumes that offer a higher degree of complexity in the kitchen, and on the table, will afford us the opportunity to explore more complex wine pairings. If you happen to be squarely in the "I know nothing of wine camp" with me, take the descriptions of the wine (flavors, notes, etc.) that Donnie has provided to a reputable wine store and they will be able to easily help you with your selections until you get the hang of it.

The Meal Pairing Matrix did prove to be quite difficult to actually fit into a book though. Trust me, it was much easier to deal with as a stand-alone file. For the purposes of printing, we have separated the matrix into two tables. The first table is the actual matrix that contains all of the menus and the dishes that make up the menu option. The second table contains serving sizes (for the gathering) and estimated costs associated with the chosen menu.

Cost and Complexity Indicator Legend

The Cost and Complexity indicators are in relation to the entire meal pairing. However, the cost indicator <u>does not include</u> the beverage. The Cost and Complexity indicators can be read as follows:

Cost
$ - Less than $80.00 for the entire menu
$$ - Less than $120.00 for the entire menu
$$$ - More than $120.00 for the entire menu

Complexity
1 - "Anyone can cook!"
2 - You know your way around the kitchen or grill
3 - Consider running a restaurant!

NOTE: Some menus do <u>not</u> contain all five of the menu items available (Appetizer, Salad/Soup, Main, Side, and Dessert). This is by design. On some menus, for varying reasons, a certain menu element is not needed. These "voids" are explained in the individual menu sections, which contain the menu pairing recipes.

Menu Name	Appetizer	Soup/Salad	Main	Side	Dessert	Red Wine	White Wine
On the Water Front	Clams Casino	Mixed Baby Green Salad w/ Raspberries and Feta	Low Country Boil	Baguette	Fresh Fruit	n/a	Dry Riesling (or Pilsner beer)
Winter's Respite	Greek Tiropetes	n/a	Stuffed Pork Tenderloin	Roasted Potatoes and Sweet Onions	Mocha Tiramisu	Merlot	n/a
South of the Border	Shrimp Ceviche'	Tortilla Soup	Pollo Al Chilindron	Quinoa Pilaf	Fried Ice Cream (optional)	Spanish Rose	Albarino
French Countryside	Pissaladière	Spinach Salad w/ Hot Bacon Dressing	Coq au Vin Fines Herbs	n/a	White Balsamic Custard Tart w/ Fresh Berries	Red Burgundy (Pinot Noir)	n/a
Fancy on a Budget	Baked Brie in Puff Pastry	n/a	Plank Baked Salmon w/ Ponzu Sauce	Grilled Sesame Asparagus	Frozen Grapes	Pinot Noir	Unoaked Chardonnay
Tour of Italy	Pancetta-Wrapped Shrimp with White Bean Olive Relish	Italian Wedding Soup	Chicken Cacciatore	Angel Hair in Olive Oil	Cannoli Filled w/ Sweetened Ricotta	Sangiovese like Chianti	n/a

Menu Name	Appetizer	Soup/Salad	Main	Side	Dessert	Red Wine	White Wine
Light Grilling	Mushroom Empanada	Spring Greens with Candied Pecans	Grilled Swordfish with Maitre'd Butter	Wild Rice Pilaf	Grilled Calypso Pineapple over Ice Cream	n/a	Chardonnay
Autumn Destination	Baba Ghanouj	Knickerbocker Bean Soup	Spinach and Feta Stuffed Chicken	Steamed Rice	Linzer Torte	n/a	Sauvignon Blanc
Provencal Summer	Olive Tapenade	n/a	Provencal Pistou Pasta	Fresh Corn Salad	Simple Wildberry Shortbread	Cotes du Rhone	Chenin Blanc
A Peppery Debate	Shrimp Gabriella	Tomato, Mozzarella, and Fresh Basil Salad	Steak Au Poivre	Roasted Red Potatoes	Poached Pears in Port Wine	Cabernet Sauvignon	n/a
Northern Exposure	Five-Minute Bruschetta	Mandarin Mixed Green Salad	Pan Seared Salmon w/ Blueberry Glaze	Spiced Quinoa Timbales	Chocolate Molten Bombe with Raspberries	n/a	Unoaked Chardonnay
Herb Garden	Rosemary Peasant Bread	Gazpacho	Braised Halibut Provencal	Cilantro Rice	Chocolate Covered Strawberries	White Burgundy - Chardonnay	n/a

MEAL PAIRING MATRIX SERVING & COST INDICATORS

The following summary table gives you a pretty good outline of what each menu entails with regard to:

- Number of guests the menu can serve
- The overall cost of the menu ($, $$, $$$) minus the beverage, and;
- The amount of complexity, or difficulty, associated with the preparation of each menu (1, 2, 3 with 3 being the most complex).

Menu Name	Servings	Cost	Complexity
On the Water Front	6 to 10	$$	1
Winter's Respite	6 to 8	$	2
South of the Border	6 to 8	$$	1.5
French Countryside	6 to 8	$	2
Fancy on a Budget	6 to 8	$	1
Tour of Italy	6 to 8	$$	2
Light Grilling	6 to 8	$$	1.5
Autumn Destination	6 to 8	$	1
Provencal Summer	6 to 8	$	1
A Peppery Debate	6 to 8	$$$	2
Northern Exposure	6 to 8	$$	2
Herb Garden	6 to 8	$	2

Pre-Prep Indicator

As you begin reading through the individual recipe chapters, you will notice that each recipe contains a Pre-Prep indicator. The Pre-Prep indicator denotes if the recipe can be made days in advance, hours in advance, or if the dish needs to be prepared and served immediately. Please use the following definitions for greater understanding when reviewing the indicator noted in each recipe.

1 – Can be made a day or two ahead of time
2 – Can be prepared a few hours ahead of time
3 – Must be prepared and served immediately

Recipe Organization

Traditionally, recipes in a cookbook group recipes by genre, or type of recipe (e.g. Breads, Soups, Seafood, etc.). However, since this not a traditional cookbook, and we have provided actual menus with recipes comprising those menus, we have opted to display our recipes according to the "Menu Name."

So, for example, if you were looking for the Clams Casino recipe, you would find it in the "On the Water Front" chapter.

Now, on to the recipes...

On the Water Front

ON THE WATER FRONT

You cannot grow up as close as I did to the Chesapeake Bay or the Atlantic Ocean for that matter, and not have some proclivity toward seafood. As children growing up in northern Virginia, and then in southern North Carolina, my three brothers and I were given the opportunity to select a birthday dinner for the family. For me, it was always seafood. Therefore, it is not at all odd, or of any great surprise, that this menu is first in the matrix.

A "Low Country Boil" is basically a Southerner's take on the New England Clam Bake but incorporates additional non-seafood items like potatoes and sausage. The red, yellow, and green peppers, as well as, the corn on the cob, add some additional color.

This recipe came to pass while my wife and I were living in Charlotte, North Carolina. We lived in southeast Charlotte in a quiet little neighborhood and the neighbors quickly inducted us into the monthly "Supper Club" rotation. As I mentioned earlier, the premise behind the Supper Club was simple. Each month, one family would host as it was rotated among the neighbors. The host would provide the location and the main course. Everyone else would either bring their favorite side or provide a dish to complement the main dish. There were "regulars" that hosted specific Supper Club months too. This is to say that some families hosted specific months due to a specialty that went well with the month or season.

A neighborhood friend, Chuck Shue, was always one of the summer months because of the Low Country Boil. I obtained the basis for this recipe simply by watching him cook this dish. You would be amazed at what you can you discern simply from paying attention.

The Low Country Boil is very much a timed dish and a somewhat strict adherence to the clock must be maintained or it will be overdone and rubbery. You can cook this on a stovetop but it is not recommended due to the pots propensity to boil over as ingredients are added. Therefore, it is highly recommended that you cook this in a deep frying pot, with a steamer basket, outdoors. This is a boiled dish, not fried, so don't be wary of the dish because the pot has the name "fry" in it.

Also, if scallops are not your thing, I have been known to substitute the scallops for King Crab Legs or whole crabs. In either case, the crab usually is pre-cooked and chilled so add the crab when you add the shrimp to warm them back up.

The Clams Casino appetizer does well to set the palette up for the main dish of Low Country Boil as it incorporates smaller doses of seafood coupled with the bacon whereas the Boil has large doses of seafood and sausage. The intermezzo of Mixed Greens with Raspberries and Feta helps to cleanse the palette with a bit of fruity goodness. You should find a nice baguette to slice to make available once the Low Country Boil is presented to the guests. The bread is used to sop up juices and functions as a utensil for those that like to pile the Boil ingredients on bread to make a little seafood Bruschetta of sorts.

Between the bread and two doses of seafood, an assortment of fresh fruit serves well as a dessert. The fresh fruit dessert has been left for you to decide on what to serve. Any assortment of berries (blackberry, red raspberry, blueberry, strawberry) will do but, for me, I like oranges and plums. Since this dish is best suited for late summer, Scott also recommends melons of all varieties. For this time of year, his favorite is peaches and pears.

This menu is definitely for the occasion where seafood is popular with guests and in-season. Therefore, before any invites are distributed, you should verify that any potential guests: a.) Do not have a seafood allergy and; b.) Thoroughly enjoy seafood.

For the wine pairing, Donnie has recommended either a Pilsner, or other light lager, and a Dry Riesling. A good pilsner serves this menu well, as does the Dry Riesling, because of fruit and mineral notes found in each.

CLAMS CASINO

Serving Size	4-6
Cost	$
Complexity	1
Pre-Prep	2 - Prepare as normal, cover and refrigerate up to 6 hours. To serve, bake at 350-degrees as normal.

Ingredients:

24 Hard-Shell Clams
2 T Parsley, minced
1/4 C Parmesan Cheese, grated
2 Garlic Cloves, minced

1/4 C Dry Breadcrumbs
1/2 t Fresh Oregano Leaves
2 T Melted Butter
6 Slices Bacon, cut in 1/4

Directions:

1. Wash clams, discarding any open (dead) clams.
2. Shuck the live clams using a clam knife and discard the top shell.
3. Again using the clam knife, loosen the clam (meat) from bottom shell.
4. Drain the shells and the meat on paper towel.
5. Heat the oven to 350-degrees.
6. In small mixing bowl, combine the remaining ingredients except for the bacon and clam meat.
7. Return clams to the bottom shell and arrange in a shallow baking pan.
8. Top each with a heaping teaspoon of crumb mixture and a piece of bacon.
9. Bake at 350-degrees for 20 to 25 minutes or until the bacon is crisp and the clams are set.

NOTE: Pour rock salt into a pan and embed the prepared clams in the rock salt, pushing down slightly, to make sure that they are level.

BABY GREENS SALAD WITH RASPBERRIES AND FETA

Serving Size	6-8
Cost	$
Complexity	1
Pre-Prep	2 – You can make this several hours ahead of time but the dressing and feta should be reserved until just before serving.

Ingredients:

9 C Mixed Salad Greens, torn
3 C Raspberries, fresh or frozen
1 C Feta Cheese, crumbled
2 T Olive Oil, or Canola Oil

2 T White Balsamic Vinegar
2 t Sugar
1/8 t Salt
Dash of Pepper

Directions:

1. In a large salad bowl, gently combine the salad greens and 2-3/4 C raspberries and feta cheese.
2. Mash the remaining berries, strain, and reserve juice and discard the seeds.
3. In a bowl, whisk the raspberry juice, oil, vinegar, sugar, salt, and pepper.
4. Drizzle over salad and gently toss to coat.

Low Country Boil

Serving Size	6-8
Cost	$
Complexity	1
Pre-Prep	2 - All of the ingredients can be cut, bagged, and ready to go when you are ready to boil the water.
Wine Pairing	The crisp fruit and mineral notes of a dry Riesling make the wine very versatile, especially with the mix of shellfish and spice in this dish.

Ingredients:

1 1/2 lb Raw Shrimp (21-25 size)
1/3 C Old Bay Seasoning
1 1/2 lb Raw Scallops (small pcs.)
1 Red Bell Pepper
1 pkg Kielbasa (pre-cooked)
1 Yellow Bell Pepper

2 lbs. Red Skinned Potatoes
1 Green Bell Pepper
4-5 Ears Sweet Corn on the Cob
1/2 T Salt
1 C Sweet Onion

Directions:

Preparation:

1. Wash and quarter the 2 lbs of potatoes.
2. Shuck and halve the corncobs.
3. Slice the Kielbasa lengthwise and then into disks diagonally.
4. Cut up the onion into large chunks.
5. Slice the peppers into strips.
6. Peel and de-vein the shrimp.

NOTE: All of the following is cooked in 25 minutes. The clock starts when the potatoes start cooking. Everything is cooked in the steamer basket inside the turkey fryer with the lid on. The water will stop boiling as you add cold items like corn, shrimp, scallops, etc. The clock continues to run even though the water is not boiling. The ingredients are still being cooked even if the water is not boiling.

Boil:

1. Fill the fryer to the max line with water, add salt, and bring to a boil.
2. Place the potatoes into the steamer basket and start the clock. Let the potatoes cook alone for 15 minutes.
3. After 15 min., add the Kielbasa.
4. 3 minutes after adding the Kielbasa, add the corn on the cob halves, peppers and onions.
5. 2 minutes after adding the corn, add the shrimp, scallops, and Old Bay seasoning.
6. Pull the steamer basket out and serve when the shrimp float (or turn pink), about 3-5 minutes.
7. Serve with a thick-cut sliced bread, preferably a baguette or French loaf.

Winter's Respite

WINTER'S RESPITE

The Winter's Respite menu really should be the "find any food substance and stuff it with other food substances" recipe but alas, that name wasn't popular with the polling community. Nevertheless, this menu is a hearty indoor meal offering plenty of sustenance on a cold blustery day.

The Greek Tiropetes and the Stuffed Pork Tenderloin will give you your daily serving of dairy in the form of cheese. The Tiropetes call for Feta and the pork calls for crumbled cheese in general. We have not specified a particular type of cheese for the pork because tastes differ and what we like you may be adverse to so pick any cheese you like and use that. Over time, you can try different cheeses until you determine what cheese best suits your palette.

The first time I made this recipe I used pre-crumbled Colby and Monterey Jack. However, given my "natural ingredients are better" soapbox from earlier in the book, I buy these two cheeses in block form and crumble it myself. Blue Cheese would do well for some but, for me, it always leaves a chalky after taste. I have also found that crumbled cheese works better than shredded cheese for the simple fact that, when cooked, shredded cheese tends to liquefy.

With a menu complexity rating of 2, one should expect, not just a higher degree of complexity, but also, more preparation time as well.

The Mocha Tiramisu recipe won't disappoint on that front. You will need plenty of time to create this masterpiece of decadent delight. The Stuffed Pork Tenderloin recipe is completed fairly quickly but this recipe offers a higher degree of complexity because we are going to fillet the pork loin open using a "book" cut, roll it out, and then stuff it with sautéed spinach and fresh crumbled cheese. Knife skills are in high demand for this to be accomplished correctly.

You may have noticed that this menu does not call for a soup or salad. This is by design. Between the chives in the Tiropetes, spinach, onions, and optional sautéed tomatoes in the pork, not to mention, an additional serving of onion, coupled with a starch in the potato side, you will receive plenty of greens and food for that matter. Therefore, a salad is not necessary. Besides, you will want to save room for the Mocha Tiramisu.

For the wine pairing, Donnie has recommended a Merlot as the subtle tannins work well with the robust flavor of the pork tenderloin.

GREEK TIROPETES

Serving Size	6-8
Cost	$
Complexity	1
Pre-Prep	1 – These can be prepared and refrigerated for up to 24 hrs. prior to cooking. These can actually be frozen and stored for 2-3 months.

Ingredients:

2 Eggs, slightly beaten
1/4 t White Pepper
1/4 C Chives, finely chopped

1 lb. Phyllo, thawed
1/4 C Butter, melted
1 lb. Feta Cheese (or finely shredded Monterey Jack)

Directions:

1. In a mixing bowl, crumble the cheese then stir in the eggs, chives, and white pepper until well mixed.
2. Layer 2 sheets phyllo with melted butter between.
3. After layering, cut lengthwise into 3 strips.
4. Place a heaping t of filling close to end of each strip, fold each strip, end over end in a triangle – like you would fold a flag... or a paper football.
5. Place on greased cookie sheet.

> *NOTE: At this point, you can refrigerate for up to 24 hours.*

6. Just before baking the Tiropetes triangles, brush them with melted butter.
7. Bake at 350-degrees, or until they are puffed and golden, for about 20 min.

STUFFED PORK TENDERLOIN

Serving Size	4-6
Cost	$
Complexity	2
Pre-Prep	2 - The spinach can be sautéed and left to cool an hour or so before you are ready to cook the loin.
Wine Pairing	The rich red fruit flavors and subtle tannins in Merlot are the perfect match for the robust flavor in this stuffed pork tenderloin.

Ingredients:

1 Large Pork Tenderloin, 1 – 2 lbs.
4 T Olive Oil
1 t Black Pepper, fresh ground
1/2 C Onion, chopped

7 oz. Baby Spinach
1 C Cheese Crumbles
1/2 t Salt
1 pt. Grape Tomatoes (optional)

Directions:

Sautéing the Spinach

1. Wash the spinach.
2. Heat 2 T of the olive oil in a large skillet over high heat.
3. Add the onion and cook for 1 minute.
4. Add the spinach, pushing it down into the skillet, and 1/8 t salt and 1/2 t pepper. Cover and cook over medium heat for about 1 1/2 minutes, until the spinach is wilted.
5. Remove the lid and cook, uncovered, until the liquid from the spinach has evaporated. Transfer to a plate and let cool.

Butterflying the Tenderloin

To butterfly the tenderloin, you will need to make parallel cuts from opposite sides of the loin. The first cut will be in the top third of the loin and the second cut will be in the bottom third of the loin. You will not cut all the way through the loin with either cut as you are merely trying to unfold the loin like a book, or a tri-fold pamphlet. Additionally, you want the loin slices to be of three equal thicknesses. Here's how:

1. Trim the tenderloin of any fat and silverskin. (Silverskin is a slippery, almost paper-thin, piece of connective tissue.)
2. Lay the loin on the cutting board so that it is perpendicular to you (i.e. pointing away from you).
3. Now, holding your knife so the blade is parallel to the loin, cut two-thirds to three-quarters of the way through the loin, at approximately the top third line of the loin, the entire length of the tenderloin stopping when you are about one-half to three-eighths of an inch from the other side.
4. Pull the piece back that you have just cut to reveal the first third of the book.
5. Now, turn the cutting board, not the tenderloin, so the uncut side is closest to your cutting hand, and place your knife on the loin where the first cut stopped. Your knife-edge should be headed the opposite direction of the end cut.
6. Now make the second cut diagonally down through the remaining loin piece away from the open book page stopping when you are about one-half to three-eighths of an inch from the other side.

The tenderloin should now open up like a book.

Cooking the Tenderloin

1. Open up the butterflied tenderloin and pound it a little to extend it to about 12 x 8 inches wide. You may need to use a rolling pin.
2. Preheat the oven to 350-degrees.
3. Arrange half the spinach mixture down the center of the butterflied tenderloin and top with the cheese.
4. Add the rest of the spinach, fold in the sides, and roll the tenderloin back and forth to evenly distribute and encase the filling.
5. Using twist ties made of aluminum foil, or cooking string, secure the tenderloin to keep it from unrolling when searing.
6. Heat the remaining 2 T oil in a large ovenproof nonstick skillet.
7. Sprinkle the outside of the tenderloin with 1/8 t salt and 1/2 t pepper.
8. Place the tenderloin carefully in the skillet and brown it, turning occasionally, for about 5 minutes.
9. Carefully remove the foil strips from the tenderloin and bake in the oven for 15-20 minutes, when it will be slightly pink in the center.
10. Transfer the tenderloin to a plate, cover, and keep warm while you prepare the tomatoes (the pork will continue to cook as it sits). Allow to rest for at least 5-7 minutes.
11. (Optional) In the skillet you browned, and cooked, the tenderloin, add the tomatoes and salt and pepper to taste.
12. (Optional) Sauté over high heat for 1 1/2 to 2 minutes, until just softened. (Add wine or water if more liquid is needed)
13. Slice the tenderloin crosswise into as many medallions as possible - about 1/2 to 3/4 inch thick depending on the total number of guests.
14. (Optional) Garnish with the sautéed tomatoes.

Roasted Potatoes and Sweet Onions

Serving Size   4-6
Cost $
Complexity   1
Pre-Prep   3 – These cannot be prepared a few hours, or a day, ahead so this recipe receives a pre-prep rating of 3 meaning it must be prepared and served immediately.

Ingredients:

4-6 Large Baking Potatoes (if using small potatoes, double the recipe)	4-5 Med. Onions, preferably Vidalia or sweet onions
1/4 t Sea Salt	Pinch of Fresh Ground Pepper
2 T Peanut or Safflower oil	

Directions:

1. Preheat oven to 400 or 425-degrees.
2. Wash potatoes and split in half lengthwise.
3. Peel onions and then thinly slice crosswise.
4. Pour oil on rimmed baking pan (spring roll pan).
5. Season the potatoes and onions with salt and pepper and place cut side down on the pan.
6. Place the pan on the bottom rack of the oven and bake for 45 minutes or until potatoes and onions are tender when pierced with a fork and dark brown on the undersides.
7. Let rest for about 5 minutes and serve.

NOTE: Ovens vary so try cooking at 400-degrees first. If they are not done in about 45 minutes, cook them at 425-degrees the next time you make them.

MOCHA TIRAMISU

Serving Size	6-8
Cost	$
Complexity	2
Pre-Prep	2 - This dessert can be made ahead of time due to the cooling step.

Ingredients:

1 (18.25 oz) pkg. of Chocolate Cake Mix, with pudding

1 Milk Chocolate Candy Bar, Ghirardelli or Hershey

2 Large Eggs

1 C Water

3/4 C Sweetened Condensed Milk (do not use evaporated milk)

1/2 C Kahlua

1/2 C Vegetable Oil

Creamy Coffee Filling

1 (8 oz) pkg. Cream Cheese, softened

2 T Kahlua

1/4 C Sweetened Condensed Milk (do not use evaporated milk)

1 1/2 C Whipping Cream, whipped

Espresso Sauce

1 T Espresso Coffee, instant

1 (14 oz) can of Sweetened Condensed Milk (do not use evaporated milk)

1/4 C Butter, or margarine

1/4 C Water, boiling

Directions:

1. Preheat oven to 350-degrees.
2. Grease 2 (8-inch) round cake pans.
3. Beat 3/4 C condensed milk, cake mix, water, eggs, and oil on low setting, in a large bowl, until blended well.
4. Now pour half of the batter into each pan.
5. Bake at 350 for 25-30 minutes and let cool in the pans on wire racks for 10 minutes.
6. Now, remove from the pans and cool.
7. Cut each cake into half (making 4 cake layers).
8. Then, make the Creamy Coffee Filling and Espresso Sauce - below.
9. Brush each layer of cake evenly with coffee liqueur.
10. Put 1 layer in a 4-qt bowl or trifle dish and drizzle with 1/3 of the Espresso Sauce.
11. Then, top with 1/3 of the Creamy Coffee Filling.
12. Repeat that process with remaining cake layers, ending with a cake layer.
13. Garnish the top with shaved chocolate (this set optional) or confectioners' sugar and chill.
14. Store the cake covered in the refrigerator.

Creamy Coffee Filling

1. In a large bowl, beat the Creamy Coffee Filling ingredients, minus the Whip Cream, until well blended.
2. Whip Cream separately then fold in the whipped cream to the creamed ingredients. (Chill, if preferred).

Espresso Sauce

1. Combine water and espresso in a small saucepan and bring to a boil.
2. Now, lower the heat and mix in condensed milk.
3. Over a medium heat, cook and stir the mixture until it reaches a boil.
4. Finally, remove it from the heat, mix in the butter, and cool.

South of the Border

SOUTH OF THE BORDER

South of the Border, to some, conjures images of the Mexican Hat Dance, refried beans, tacos, and Montezuma's Revenge. To others it represents a proud culture with exceptional cuisine. We have drawn inspiration from the latter for this menu.

The Tortilla Soup and Pollo al Chilindron consume a great number of ingredients and this is typical in Spanish themed meals. It is the combination of many ingredients that provides this culture with its unique flavors and textures. Review the ingredient list for each recipe as it is quite possible that you will be headed to the store for a few of these items.

First, we start you off with an extremely straightforward Ceviche' recipe. Traditionally, a Ceviche' is made with raw seafood but in this case we call for pre-cooked shrimp so we can serve it cold. So for those squeamish about raw fish, fear not. It's already cooked. The Tortilla Soup can be made ahead of time and served while the Chilindron is cooking.

The Pollo al Chilindron, as I mentioned earlier, was one of the first dishes to inspire me in some time. Therefore, I thought it only fitting to include my interpretation here. The Chilindron is being served with a Quinoa Pilaf. Think of quinoa as a rice side and you can quickly see where we are headed with these two dishes being combined. There will be many juices and flavors seeping from the Chilindron and the quinoa will aid in the collection of those flavors.

For dessert, we couldn't resist using the fryer and have provided a Fried Ice Cream recipe for you and your guests to enjoy. An exceptionally cold freezer will aid you in the execution of this recipe.

Donnie has provided us with two wines for this menu selection. The Spanish Albarino or Dry Rose will highlight the flavors of the Pollo al Chilindron. To further enhance the meal, cook with the wine you are drinking.

SHRIMP CEVICHE'

Serving Size	6-10
Cost	$
Complexity	1
Pre-Prep	2 – Can be made several hours ahead of time.

Ingredients:

3 lbs Shrimp, cooked, peeled, and deveined
2 Large Tomatoes, diced
4 Limes, squeezed
1 Red Onion, diced

1 Serrano Pepper (or Jalapeno), seeded and minced
1 Bunch Cilantro, diced
2 Large Avocados, diced
2 Lemons, squeezed
1 Large Cucumber, peeled and diced

Directions:

1. Cut shrimp into 1-inch pieces and add to bowl.
2. Add the citrus juice and begin cutting the rest of the Ceviche' ingredients.
3. You may want to drain half of the juice off if you don't want a strong lemon / lime overtone of flavor.
4. Add red onion, tomatoes, chilies, and cilantro and allow the ingredients to marry their flavors.
5. Add avocados and cucumber before serving.
6. Serve with corn chips for dipping.

TORTILLA SOUP

Serving Size	6-8
Cost	$
Complexity	1
Pre-Prep	2 – Can be made several hours ahead of time and re-heated on the stovetop.

Ingredients:

1 C Carrot, diced	1/8 t Salt
2 (15 oz.) can of Tomatoes, diced	1 pkg. Corn Tortillas, crushed - 10 ct
1 C Celery	1/4 t Pepper
1 (6 oz.) can of Green Chilies, diced	1 C Milk
1 C Onion, diced	2 T Corn Oil
1 packet of Taco Seasoning	7 C Chicken Stock
1 Clove Garlic, diced	Cilantro, chopped
12 oz. Chicken Meat, poached and diced	12 oz. Monterey Jack Cheese, shredded

Directions:

1. Sauté carrots, onions, celery, garlic, and salt and pepper in corn oil until tender.
2. Add chicken broth and bring to a boil.
3. Add tomatoes, chilies, taco seasoning, and chicken.
4. Cut Tortillas into small pieces and add to broth mixture.
5. Let boil for 20 minutes or until tortillas are thoroughly incorporated into soup stirring occasionally to keep from sticking.
6. Reduce heat, add 8 oz. of cheese, then simmer for 10 minutes.
7. Add milk and simmer for additional 10 minutes.
8. If thicker soup is desired, add more diced tortillas and let incorporate into soup.
9. Garnish with shredded cheese, cilantro, and broken tortilla chips.

POLLO AL CHILINDRON

Serving Size	6-8
Cost	$
Complexity	1 – Even though it has a higher than normal ingredient count, it is still relatively easy to make.
Pre-Prep	1 – This stew can be made a day or two ahead of time and slowly re-heated for 30 minutes prior to serving. We recommend slow cooking so this is a good excuse to break out the crock-pot and replace the breasts with thighs.
Wine Pairing	The raciness of a Spanish Albarino or Dry Rose will highlight the flavors of this delicious stew. If you go with the white wine, cook with the wine you are drinking.

Ingredients:

1/4 C Extra Virgin Olive Oil, plus 3 T
1 C Tomato Sauce
2 C Onion, diced
Salt and pepper to taste
1 C Prosciutto, thin and diced
2 t Oregano
1 C Green Bell Pepper, diced
2 T Black Olives, sliced
4 Chicken Breasts, each breast quartered (for more flavor, try 6 bone-in chicken thighs)

1 C Canned Navy Beans
2 T Garlic, minced
1 Fresh Rosemary Sprig
1 C Dry White Wine
1 Bay Leaf
1/2 t Paprika
1 C Red Bell Pepper, diced
2 C Chicken Stock
4 Tomatoes, peeled, seeded, and chopped

Directions:

1. Heat 1 T of the olive oil in a 12-quart pot over medium-high heat.
2. Season the chicken pieces with salt then brown them on all sides – may need to brown them in batches.
3. Transfer the chicken to a platter and set aside.
4. Add the 1/4 C of olive oil to the same pot, and when the oil is hot, add the onions and peppers.
5. Reduce the heat to low and cook slowly until the vegetables are dark golden brown, about 30 minutes. (Add 1 T of stock if the onions start to burn.)
6. Add the garlic and cook for 5 more minutes.
7. Add the white wine and cook until it evaporates, 4 to 5 minutes.
8. Add the Prosciutto and browned chicken pieces, as well as any juices that have collected, and cook for 5 more minutes.
9. Stir in the remaining ingredients: paprika, tomatoes, tomato sauce, black olives, oregano, navy beans, rosemary, bay leaf, and stock and simmer over low heat for 1 hour or until the chicken is cooked completely through.
10. Season to taste with salt before serving.

QUINOA PILAF

Serving Size   6-8
Cost $
Complexity   1
Pre-Prep   3 – prepare and serve immediately

Ingredients:

1 C Quinoa, well rinsed and uncooked

2 T Olive Oil

1 t Ground Cumin

1 Small Onion, minced

1 Bay Leaf

1/4 C Red Bell Pepper, diced

2 C Vegetable Stock (or Chicken Stock)

Sea Salt and Pepper to taste

1/4 C Green Bell Pepper, diced

2 T Cilantro, fresh and chopped

2 Garlic Cloves, minced

Directions:

1. Cook onions in olive oil until edges turn brown.
2. Add peppers and garlic to onions and stir for 30 seconds, and then stir in Quinoa and cumin.
3. Continue to stir for about a minute then add broth, bay leaf and salt and pepper to taste.
4. Simmer on stove with a lid until quinoa is soft or place in a 350-degree oven for about 20 minutes.
5. Serve after stirring in chopped fresh cilantro.

FRIED ICE CREAM

Serving Size	As Needed
Cost	$
Complexity	2
Pre-Prep	2 – The ice cream balls can be prepared and breaded many hours, if not days, ahead of time.

Ingredients:

1 qt. Vanilla Ice Cream
3 C Crushed Cornflakes Cereal
1 t Ground Cinnamon

3 Egg Whites
2 qts. Vegetable Oil for Frying

Directions:

1. Scoop ice cream into 8 - 1/2 C sized balls.
2. Place on baking sheet and freeze until firm, about 1 hour.
3. In a shallow dish, combine cornflakes and cinnamon.
4. In another dish, beat egg whites until foamy.
5. Roll ice cream balls in egg whites, then in cornflakes, covering ice cream completely. Repeat if necessary.
6. Freeze again until firm, at least 3 hours.
7. In deep fryer or large, heavy saucepan, heat oil to 375-degrees.
8. Using a basket or slotted spoon, fry ice cream balls 1 or 2 at a time, for 10 to 15 seconds, until golden.
9. Drain quickly on paper towels and serve immediately.

French Countryside

FRENCH COUNTRYSIDE

Take a stroll through the French countryside and enjoy this menu offering when possible. The French countryside, or any countryside for that matter, tends to win over visitors with their ability to make hearty meals from just about anything. Typically, countryside faire utilizes seasonal ingredients and is aimed at replenishing farmers, peasants, and hunters after a long day in the fields and woods.

Don't fear the fancy Pissaladière name though, as this is basically a margherita style pizza on puff pastry. Scott was turned on to this French style pizza by one of his mentors, Maurice Laudu. The story goes that Maurice was going to make this French style pizza for the two of them for lunch one day. Scott, the skeptic, asked, "Is there such a thing as French pizza?" Maurice gave Scott the classic French shrug as if he had just asked the dumbest question ever and flatly stated, "Get busy and caramelize some chopped onions." Given Scott's love affair with the caramelized onion, Scott's new favorite pizza was discovered.

The Coq au Vin dish is best cooked long and slow. If you can do this, you will be so much happier with the outcome. The longer it cooks, the more time is allowed for the flavors to marry. If you have a crock-pot, you might want to consider using it for Coq au Vin. The "Fines Herbs" of the Coq au Vin is a very French aspect to this style of cooking. Basically, fines herbs is a combination of many green herbs like parsley, tarragon, chives, and chervil. The combination of these herbs is a mainstay for southern French cooking. Believe it or not, France does border the Mediterranean.

The custard tart is not difficult but it is very step heavy and will take some time to prepare. The good news here is that the tarts can be made several hours ahead of time and refrigerated. You will find a new favorite in the Balsamic Custard Tart.

Donnie has paired only a red wine with this menu. The reasoning is that the classic nature of the Coq au Vin dish is complemented best by berry and earth tones which are readily available in a Pinot Noir, especially Burgundy.

Pissaladière

Serving Size	6-8
Cost	$
Complexity	1
Pre-Prep	2 – The onions can be caramelized ahead of time if you like.

Ingredients:

2 T Butter
1 Sheet Puff Pastry, thawed
6 Yellow Onions, chopped
1/2 C Parmesan
1/4 t Salt
4 Sliced Plum Tomatoes

1/4 t Black Pepper
1/2 t Dried Thyme
2 t Olive Oil
2 t Balsamic Vinegar
2 t Fresh Thyme, chopped
20 Black Olives in Oil, drained and sliced

Directions:

1. Melt the butter in a large skillet over medium heat.
2. Add the onions and sauté, stirring frequently, until the onions become tender and start to turn golden.
3. Sprinkle with salt, pepper, and thyme. Stir the mixture.
4. Cook for 10-15 minutes on medium high heat, stirring occasionally, until the onions are wilted, very soft, and are a medium gold throughout.
5. Add the vinegar during the last 5 minutes of cooking.
6. Remove the onions from the stove and set them aside while preparing the pastry for the Pissaladière until they reach room temperature.

7. Set the oven temperature to 425-degrees.
8. Press the thawed pastry into a rectangle on a 12 x 18-inch baking sheet, building it up a bit around the edges.
9. Spread the pastry with the onion confit, leaving 1 inch of dough uncovered around the edges of the pastry.
10. Sprinkle Parmesan over onion mixture.
11. Arrange the tomato slices and olives on the Pissaladière.
12. Bake it for 15 to 25 minutes, until the pastry has puffed up, turned golden, and crisped.
13. Remove the Pissaladière from the oven and sprinkle the olive oil and fresh thyme across the hot surface of the tart.
14. Cut it into rectangles and serve very warm or at room temperature.

SPINACH SALAD WITH HOT BACON DRESSING

Serving Size   6-8
Cost $
Complexity   1
Pre-Prep   2 – You can pre-prep by making the bacon and reserving the 2 T of Bacon Fat ahead of time.

Ingredients:

9-10 oz. Baby Spinach	2 T Cider Vinegar
8 pcs Thick-Cut Bacon	2 T Bacon Fat
1/2 C Onion, sliced	Salt and Pepper to taste
1 Garlic Clove	2 t Honey

Directions:

1. Put the spinach in a large bowl. The spinach will shrink down some in the hot dressing, but you will need the room to work.
2. Chop the bacon and fry until crisp.
3. Remove with slotted spoon and drain on paper towels.

NOTE: If you like a lightly dressed salad, leave about 2 T of the bacon fat in the pan. If you want more dressing, then leave more bacon fat in the pan and balance it with additional vinegar and honey. (This dressing is a sweet and sour sort of thing.)

---

4. Cook the onion in the fat for 2-3 minutes.
5. Add the garlic - cook for 15-30 seconds or until it is starting to be fragrant. Be careful not to brown the garlic or it will get bitter.
6. Add the vinegar, and scrape up the brown bits in the pan. (The vinegar will seem potent, but it mellows quickly with the heat and honey.)
7. Add the salt and pepper then stir to dissolve.
8. Pour the dressing over the spinach.
9. Toss the spinach (tongs work well) until coated.
10. Transfer to individual plates or bowls and top with bacon bits and other toppings as desired.

Coq Au Vin Fines Herbs

Serving Size	6-8
Cost	$
Complexity	1.5
Pre-Prep	2 – This dish is made several hours ahead and allowed to marry for a long period of time.
Wine Pairing	This classic dish screams for the bright berry and earth tones of a Pinot Noir, especially Burgundy.

Ingredients:

8 Chicken Thighs, bone in
1/2 C Grape Tomatoes, sliced
2 t Olive Oil
1/2 Stick of Butter
2 T Shallots, chopped

1/2 C White Wine
1 C Chicken Stock
Black Pepper, fresh ground
Arugula
1/4 C Fresh Herbs, finely chopped (chives, parsley, etc.)

Directions:

1. Heat a large sturdy skillet (not non-stick).
2. Brush both sides of chicken with olive oil and place them in the hot skillet.
3. Cook for 2 to 3 minutes over fairly high heat on each side (searing).
4. Remove chicken from pan and place on a plate.
5. Add shallots to the pan and sauté until lightly browned.
6. Add wine stirring constantly releasing the encrusted juices from the pan back into the liquid.
7. Add butter and herbs to the liquid in the pan and cook for a few seconds.

8. Add chicken back into the pan, add the tomatoes, and stock. At this point, you can cook this one of three different ways.
    a. Cover and cook on lowest possible setting on your stovetop for 2 hours.
    b. Cover and place in your oven at 300-degrees for about 45 minutes to 2 hours.
    c. Place all of the ingredients into a crock-pot and cook on low for 4 to 6 hours.

---

*NOTE: Do **not** stir during the cooking process. The chicken will become extremely tender and fall off of the bone. Therefore, be careful serving this as well or the chicken will wind up on the floor.*

---

9. Serve over Arugula.

White Balsamic Custard Tart with Fresh Berries

Serving Size	6-8
Cost	$
Complexity	2
Pre-Prep	2 – You can make this up to 4 hrs ahead of time but any earlier and the tarts will become soggy.

Ingredients:

Crust

1 1/4 C All Purpose Flour
1 Large Egg Yolk
3 T Sugar

1 T Whipping Cream
1/4 t Salt
1/2 C Butter (chilled & unsalted), cut into 1/2 in. cubes

Filling

1/2 C Whipping Cream
3/4 C Water
2 T Cornstarch
3/4 C Sugar
2 Large Eggs
1/4 C Unsalted Butter (1/2 stick)

4 Large Egg Yolks
1 t Vanilla Extract
2 1/2 pt. Blueberries
1/2 C White Balsamic Vinegar
1 1/2 pt. Raspberries
2 Large Strawberries, hulled and sliced

Directions:

Crust

1. Combine flour, sugar, and salt in processor; blend 5 seconds.
2. Add butter and blend, using on/off turns, until a coarse meal forms. (It should look little like yellow peas.)
3. Add egg yolk and cream.
4. Using on/off turns, blend until moist clumps form.
5. Gather dough into ball.
6. Press dough evenly into 9-inch-diameter tart pan with removable bottom.
7. Pierce dough all over with fork.
8. Preheat oven to 375-degrees.
9. Bake crust until golden, pressing with back of fork if crust bubbles, about 20 minutes, and then let cool.

Filling

1. Stir cream and cornstarch in medium bowl until cornstarch dissolves.
2. Add eggs, egg yolks, and vanilla; whisk to blend.
3. Boil vinegar in heavy medium saucepan until reduced to 1/4 C, about 3 minutes.
4. Add 3/4 C water, sugar, and butter.
5. Stir until butter melts; return to boil.
6. Gradually whisk vinegar mixture into egg mixture; return to pan.
7. Whisk until custard thickens and boils, about 1 minute.
8. Strain into bowl and allow the filling to cool.
9. Spread custard in prepared crust.
10. Cover and chill tart at least 3 hours and up to 1 day.

Topping

1. Arrange strawberries, raspberries, and blue berries on top of tart.

Fancy on a Budget

FANCY ON A BUDGET

Not only is this menu a budget conscience menu but it is also incredibly easy to prepare. The toughest part of this menu is grilling the asparagus or perhaps caramelizing the onion for the Baked Brie.

Baking the Brie in the manner we have described provides for a unique, or elegant, form of presentation. The same can be said for the Plank Baked Salmon and Grilled Asparagus. Not many people are brave enough to try and cook on cedar but it is relatively easy to accomplish. Do yourself a favor though. Go to the home improvement store and buy a length of cedar plank and cut it yourself. Purchasing pre-cut planks from the grocery or kitchen store is not a very efficient use of money. You can get a 1x4x8 piece of lumber for the same amount of money, $5.00 - $7.00, and the larger stores will cut it for you for free. Rough-cut lumber will be closer to the actual dimensions mentioned but a milled board (smooth) will be 1/4 – 1/2 inch smaller in thickness and width. Under no circumstances should you use the green pressure treated lumber for anything other than construction purposes.

You may smell the cedar burning/smoking. This is normal. It will not catch fire because it has been soaked in water. The baking of the salmon on the cedar, and the inevitable smoking of the cedar plank, provides and extra bit of unique flavor to the salmon. You can present the salmon to your guests on the cedar plank or remove it to a plate. Garnish either presentation method with the asparagus. Even though there are some French undertones in this menu offering, the Ponzu sauce is a traditional sauce used in Asian cooking and complements the salmon and asparagus well.

The asparagus has a great deal of possibility when it comes to presentation because it basically resembles a "Linkin Log." Use your imagination with the asparagus and how it can be incorporated into a Haute Cuisine themed event. We have provided you with the option of presenting the asparagus as rafts but if your event or imagination takes you somewhere else, go with it.

Since the theme here is "fancy on a budget" we thought long and hard about a fitting dessert. We eventually landed on Frozen Grapes. Frozen Grapes served in finger bowls will definitely add to the menu theme of "Fancy on a Budget."

As for the wine pairing, you have the option of choosing between a red and a white. The Pinot Noir and the salmon is a classic pairing but the Chardonnay will do wonders with salmon in this instance due to the use of the cedar plank.

BAKED BRIE IN PUFF PASTRY

Serving Size   6-8
Cost $
Complexity   1
Pre-Prep   1 – The Brie can be wrapped in the puff pastry a day ahead of time and refrigerated. Once it is baked though, you need to serve it immediately.

Ingredients:

1/2 pkg. (17.5 oz) Frozen Puff Pastry, thawed
1 Med. Onion (Preferably Vidalia)
1 8 oz. Wheel of Brie Cheese

1 Green Apple (Granny Smith), peeled and sliced
1/4 C Almonds, sliced
1 Egg

Directions:

1. Preheat oven to 350-degrees.
2. Lightly grease a 9-inch pie pan.
3. Caramelize sliced onions in a sauté pan with Olive Oil.
4. When evenly browned, add sliced apples and continue to cook until the apple slices are limp. Set aside to cool for at least 15 -20 minutes
5. Slice the wheel of Brie in half, horizontally, so that the halves are two, flatter wheels of Brie.
6. Lay the puff pastry in the pie pan.
7. Place half of the Brie (rind-side down) onto the pastry dough.
8. Sprinkle almonds evenly over the top.
9. Place the other half of the Brie (rind-side up) over the almonds.
10. Top the Brie with the onion and apple mixture.
11. Bundle the pastry dough around the Brie.
12. Brush beaten egg over pastry dough.
13. Bake for 15 to 20 minutes.
14. Let cool for 5 minutes before serving.

PLANK BAKED SALMON WITH PONZU SAUCE

Serving Size	6 servings
Cost	$
Complexity	1.5
Pre-Prep	1 – The Ponzu Sauce can be made a day earlier than needed – cover and refrigerate.
Wine Pairing	While Pinot Noir and salmon is a traditional pairing, a rich Chardonnay can be magical with salmon off the plank. Fully cook the asparagus to prevent the wine from tasting vegetal.

Ingredients:

6 Salmon Fillets (7 or 8 oz)
1 C Orange Juice
2 T Lime Juice, fresh squeezed
1/2 C Sake

1/4 t Crushed Red Pepper, dried
1/4 C Sugar
2 t Water
1/4 C Soy Sauce
1 1/2 t Cornstarch

Directions:

1. Soak the cedar plank in water for 20 minutes or longer before using.
2. Combine orange juice, sake, sugar, soy sauce, lime juice, and red pepper in a small, but heavy, saucepan.
3. Bring to a boil over medium-high heat, stirring until sugar dissolves and until the mixture is reduced to 1 1/3 C, about 5 minutes.
4. Combine 2 t water and cornstarch in small bowl, stirring until cornstarch dissolves.
5. Add cornstarch mixture to Ponzu sauce and boil until sauce thickens and is clear, stirring frequently, about 1 minute.
6. Preheat oven to 400-degrees and brush each of the salmon fillets with 1 T of the Ponzu sauce.
7. Bake salmon, skin side down, for 5 minutes.
8. Remove the salmon fillets and brush each fillet with another T of the Ponzu sauce.
9. Bake until salmon is just cooked through, about 5 minutes.

NOTE: You may smell the cedar burning/smoking. This is normal. It will not catch fire because it has been soaked in water. The smoking of the cedar plank provides and extra bit of flavor to the salmon.

GRILLED SESAME ASPARAGUS

Serving Size	6-8
Cost	$
Complexity	1
Pre-Prep	2/3 – If making rafts, the toothpicks, or skewers, need to be soaked for at least an hour. If not, prepare and serve immediately.

> *NOTE: You can serve these grilled asparagus as individual stalks or as little rafts of asparagus. To make the rafts, perform the steps denoted as "Optional" below.*

Ingredients:

1 Garlic Clove, minced

1 lb Asparagus

2 T Sesame Seeds

2 T Sesame Oil (dark Sesame Oil works too if you prefer that taste)

1 T Soy Sauce

Salt and Pepper to taste

Wooden toothpicks or bamboo skewers (optional)

Directions:

1. In a shallow pan, soak skewers in cold water for 1 hour, then drain and set aside. (Optional)
2. Preheat grill to high.
3. Remove the woody bases of the asparagus and discard.
4. Skewer 4 or 5 asparagus spears together, using the toothpicks or 2 bamboo skewers (it will look like a raft). (Optional)
5. In a small bowl, combine the sesame oil, soy sauce, and garlic and stir with a fork to mix.
6. Brush this mixture on the asparagus on both sides.
7. Season the asparagus with a little salt and lots of pepper.
8. When ready to cook, place the asparagus on the hot grate and grill until nicely browned on both sides, 2 to 4 minutes.
9. Sprinkle with the sesame seeds as they grill.

You can serve the asparagus as rafts or un-skewered.

FROZEN GRAPES

Serving Size	As Needed
Cost	$
Complexity	1
Pre-Prep	2 - These SHOULD be prepared a few hours ahead of time as they need to be frozen but not rock solid. If prepared a few days ahead of time, remove them from the freezer about 5-10 minutes before serving.

Ingredients:

1 Bunch Seedless Red Grapes   1 Bunch Seedless Green Grapes

Directions:

1. Separate all grapes from the stem.
2. Wash grapes in a colander under running water.
3. Dry all grapes really well.
4. Line a large baking pan with parchment paper.
5. Place the washed and dried grapes in a single layer – try to keep the grapes from touching as best you can.
6. Place the pan in freezer until ready to serve.
7. To serve, remove grapes from parchment and serve in bowls.

Tour of Italy

TOUR OF ITALY

Much like the French Countryside menu, the Tour of Italy offers you and your gathering a taste of the simpler life. This simpler life is often associated with smaller towns and villages found in rural or more agrarian areas of certain countries. A complement to that simpler life is the style of cooking. Fresh ingredients that are in season and grown locally in, and around, the towns and villages are often what constitutes the ingredients list in dishes, like a Cacciatore.

The term "Cacciatore" is an Italian term for "hunter" and is typical of the meals served in the countryside of Italy. However, Italy has much more to offer and we have tried to represent that in the Pancetta Wrapped Shrimp with White Bean Olive Relish, the Italian Wedding Soup, and the Angel Hair in Olive Oil. Many of the more notable Italian exports, like olives, cured meats, pastas, and desserts are reflected in the Tour of Italy menu as well.

This menu does require a little bit of prep and some of this prep can be accomplished a day ahead of time. Pre-prepping the relish for the shrimp, soup, and the cannoli shells for the dessert can save you a great deal of time in the kitchen the day of the gathering. The rest of the menu offering needs to be made the day of. The guests will definitely go home happy, full, and satisfied.

The Pancetta-Wrapped Shrimp with White Bean Olive Relish adds a slight increase to the degree of difficulty. This is mostly due to the amount of prep needed to present this dish more than anything else.

The Italian Wedding Soup is a staple in our household and there are a great many variations that can be utilized here. Feel free to experiment with the meat combinations used to make the meatballs. I have tried turkey and ground beef/sirloin, sausage and turkey, sausage and ground beef/sirloin, and even ground chicken with sausage or beef or turkey. No matter your preference, here's a trick. Bake the meatballs before adding them to the soup. This will keep them from breaking down when the soup is stirred by an overzealous pot-stirring spouse.

Also, there are two sides when it comes to making Italian Wedding Soup. One side says the soup contains noodles, or a bit of pasta, and one side says it doesn't. Determine your preference and make it however you see fit.

The Chicken Cacciatore is not all that dissimilar to the Coq au Vin dish from the French Countryside menu except it doesn't cook for as long. We don't want the chicken to break down so 30 minutes of cook time is all that is needed after browning. Fresh Angel Hair in Olive Oil served with the cacciatore works well with the sauce and seasonings attached to the chicken.

What's more Italian than a cannoli I ask you? The only thing missing from this recipe is the little Italian grandmother handing you the generations old recipe. The first time you make these you might want to prepare yourself for failure. Making a cannoli shell takes a bit of practice but, much like the "riding a bike" metaphor, once you get the hang of it, you'll blow right through that forevermore.

For the wine pairing, Donnie recommends the dried berry notes and acidity of a Sangiovese. This is especially true for a Sangiovese from Chianti.

PANCETTA-WRAPPED SHRIMP WITH WHITE BEAN OLIVE RELISH

Serving Size	4
Cost	$
Complexity	2
Pre-Prep	2 / 3 – The wrapping of the shrimp with the pancetta can be done a few hours ahead of time and the Olive Relish can be made the day before.

Ingredients:

For the Shrimp:

8 Shrimp (U-12 size), peeled and de-veined

8 slices Pancetta, thin

For the Relish:

3 oz. White Beans, cooked
4 Basil Leaves, fresh
2 Fresh Lemons, juiced
1 Red Bell Pepper, roasted and chopped
4 oz. Black Olives, pitted and chopped

3 T Extra Virgin Olive Oil
Salt and Pepper to taste
Grated Zest from 1/2 Lemon
1 Yellow Bell Pepper, roasted and chopped
4 Radicchio Cups

Directions:

1. Clean and wrap each shrimp with a slice of pancetta.
2. Grill the shrimp on medium heat and make sure that the pancetta is crisp – if grilled with any higher heat, the pancetta will flame up.
3. Combine and toss the beans, olives, peppers, lemon zest, basil, lemon juice, olive oil, salt, and pepper.
4. Fill the radicchio cup with the relish.
5. Place two grilled shrimp on top of the relish filled cup and serve.

Italian Wedding Soup

Serving Size	6-8
Cost	$
Complexity	2 – The first time you make it
Pre-Prep	1 – The entire soup can be made a day ahead of time. However, once the meatballs have been added, you must be careful stirring as over stirring will break down the meatballs.

Ingredients:

1 C Parmesan (or Romano Cheese) + 1/2 C for topping
1/2 lb. Ground Veal
1/2 lb. Ground Sausage
1 Large Egg
1/2 C Breadcrumbs

1 Small Head Of Escarole, washed, trimmed and chopped
Salt And Pepper to taste
2 T Parsley, finely chopped
8 C Homemade Chicken Stock

Directions:

1. Heat the broth in a large pot.
2. Combine meats, cheese, egg, bread crumbs, parsley, salt, and pepper.
3. Once the broth is hot, reduce it to a simmer.
4. Form small meatballs about one inch in diameter, and drop them into the broth.
5. Cook for about 5 minutes, and then drop in the escarole.
6. Cook for a few more minutes or until all the meatballs float to the top, and the escarole is wilted.
7. Skim off any foam that develops as the meatballs cook.
8. Serve the soup in individual bowls, with a good helping of grated cheese on top.

NOTE: The escarole can be replaced by spinach if preferred.

CHICKEN CACCIATORE

Serving Size	6-8
Cost	$
Complexity	2
Pre-Prep	2 – Can be made 2-3 hours ahead of guest arrival. Do not over stir as the chicken will break down.
Wine Pairing	The dried berry notes and acidity of a Sangiovese, especially from Chianti, partner extremely well with the flavors of the Chicken Cacciatore.

Ingredients:

1 Chicken, cut into 8 pieces (3-4 lbs.)
2 T Olive Oil
1/2 C Chicken Stock
1 Medium Onion, chopped
1 t Dried Oregano
2 Cloves Garlic, minced
1/4 C Fresh Parsley, chopped

1 (14 oz) can of Chopped Tomatoes
1 Celery Stalk, chopped
Salt and Pepper to taste
4 oz. Mushrooms, chopped
Pinch of Red Pepper Flakes
1/2 C Dry White Wine

Directions:

1. Rinse the chicken pieces, and then pat dry.
2. Heat the oil in a large skillet over medium heat, and brown the chicken pieces well on both sides.
3. Remove the chicken pieces to a plate.
4. Add the mushrooms, onions and celery to the pan drippings, and sauté until soft, about 5 minutes.
5. Add the garlic, and cook for another minute or two.
6. Add the chicken back into the skillet, and add the white wine.
7. Cook on medium heat until the wine has almost completely evaporated.

8. Add in the chopped tomatoes, broth, and seasonings.
9. Simmer, covered for about 30 minutes.

> *NOTE: If the sauce has not thickened, remove the chicken pieces from the pan, and bring the sauce mixture to a boil. Cook it for a few minutes until it has reduced and thickened. Serve hot!*

Variation: You may add some small tasty black olives to the chicken and sauce mixture in the last minute or two of cooking. This will add a nice little additional flavor and a contrasting color.

ANGEL HAIR IN OLIVE OIL

Serving Size	As Needed
Cost	$
Complexity	1
Pre-Prep	3 – Technically you could make this ahead of time but freshly prepared pasta is better. This is where the finer, more expensive, olive oils actually make a palatable difference.

Ingredients:

1 pkg. (16 oz) Angel Hair Pasta   1 T Extra Virgin Olive Oil
1 T Salt

Directions:

1. Fill a large pot with water
2. Season the water with 1 T salt.
3. When the water begins boiling, add the angel hair.
4. Stir regularly in beginning to ensure that pasta doesn't clump.
5. Check pasta after cooking for about 5 minutes for doneness.
6. Strain and drizzle with olive oil before serving.

CANNOLI FILLED WITH SWEETENED RICOTTA

Serving Size   Makes 10-12 Cannoli's
Cost $
Complexity   1.5
Pre-Prep   1 / 2 – It is highly recommended that you make the cannoli shells the day before but do not stuff them more than 4 hours before hand.

Ingredients:

Cannoli Dough

1 1/3 C Flour	1/2 t Sugar
1 T Butter	1 Egg White, beaten
Pinch of Salt	Oil, for frying
Marsala Wine	1 T Orange Rind (or Lemon), grated

Filling

1 lb. Ricotta Cheese	2 T Sugar
2 T Semi Sweet Chocolate Chips	Fruit, slivered
1 T Candied Citron, or glazed	

NOTE: You can replace the chocolate chips with shaved semi-sweet chocolate if you prefer.

Directions:

Cannoli Dough

1. Combine flour, salt, sugar, citrus rind, and butter and blend well.
2. Add Marsala by the teaspoon until the dough is stiff.
3. Chill for 2 hours.
4. Roll dough on a lightly floured board into a large rectangle.
5. Cut into 4" ovals, or circles.
6. Wrap ovals around cannoli tubes so that the dough is wrapped lengthwise.
7. Brush the touching ends with egg white so that they will stick together.
8. Deep fry in hot oil until golden.
9. Let cool, then remove from tubes and fill when ready to serve. If not filling immediately, refrigerate the tubes.

> *NOTE: If you don't have cannoli tubes, make 2" diameter tubes out of heavy-duty aluminum foil and fold dough accordingly.*

Filling

1. Combine all of the "Filling" ingredients and fill the cannoli.

Light Grilling

LIGHT GRILLING

Previously, I mentioned taking classes through Lifelong Learning. I even provided the write-ups for the first classes I attended. There were so many classes to choose from that it was difficult to know where to start. Fortunately, Scott, and others, teaches a variety of classes to aid the would-be chef in their endeavors. There are classes that are geared toward soups, stocks, sauces, and sautéing (all of these topics will be covered in Volume II as part of a "Back to Basics" section). However, Scott also provides some grilling classes for the part-time outdoor chef to enjoy. We would be remiss if we didn't include a little of Scott's outdoor cooking expertise as part of Volume I though. To that end, we have included a fairly straightforward menu for you and your guests to enjoy by way of this Light Grilling menu.

We do recognize that the Mushroom Empanada is not a grilled appetizer but we felt that it would complement the menu well so we have selected this as the appetizer. Also, the Empanada can be made months in advance and pulled out of the freezer and served in relatively short order. The Spring Greens with Fresh Berries, Candied Pecans, and Bleu Cheese salad offers a touch of sweetness before the main course via the candied pecans. If you can make the candied pecans a day or two before the gathering, it will drastically reduce your day-of prep. Do not freeze the pre-prepped pecans as they will pick up any flavors in the freezer quickly.

The main course of Grilled Swordfish with Maître 'd Butter is a quick meal that requires little more than attentive grilling skills. This is "light" grilling after all. You are probably wondering about the butter we have denoted as part of the recipe title. Typically, the butter used is not something noted in this regard. However, when the chef has prepared the meal with a "compound butter" it will generally make the marquee. The reasoning and detail behind a compound butter is better left for Volume II but suffice it to say that a compound butter is made up of more than milk or cream. A compound butter, or beurre composé in French, is a unique mixture of butter and other ingredients. The other ingredients aid the butter in enhancing the flavor of a particular dish much like a sauce. One of these butters is probably at the heart of some of your favorite restaurant meals.

The Wild Rice Pilaf takes about 45 minutes to an hour to prepare. While the rice varietals are cooking, the salad can be prepared and Empanadas warmed and served. Once the rice is ready, throw the swordfish on the grill and dinner is soon served. Leave the grill running on low because you will need it again for the Grilled Calypso Pineapple over Ice Cream. If you have a side burner, you can prepare the sauce there as a guest prepares the pineapple as a bit of interactive fun.

Through it all, Donnie recommends that you serve a Gruner Veltliner. The characteristics of the Gruner Veltliner will help to bring out the grilled nature of the fish and the compound butter it was brushed with.

MUSHROOM EMPANADA

Serving Size	6-8
Cost	$
Complexity	1
Pre-Prep	1 – Can be made 2-3 months ahead of time and frozen.

Ingredients:

2 Medium Onions, finely chopped

6 T Unsalted Butter

1 1/2 lbs. Mushrooms, finely chopped

2 Small Red Bell Peppers, finely chopped

1/3 C Cream

1 (6-ounce) piece Serrano Ham or Prosciutto, trimmed, chopped, fine

3 T Fine Dry Breadcrumbs

Sherry

1/2 C Packed Fresh Parsley, washed, dried, and minced

Egg wash (beat 1 large egg with 1 t water)

Salt & Black Pepper, fresh ground

1 (17 1/4 oz.) pkg. Frozen Puff Pastry Sheets (2 pastry sheets), thawed

Directions:

1. In a 12-inch heavy skillet set over medium heat, cook onions in butter, stirring occasionally, until softened.
2. Stir in mushrooms and bell peppers and cook over moderate heat, stirring occasionally, until liquid mushrooms give off is evaporated and mixture begins to brown.
3. Add ham and Sherry and cook, stirring, until liquid is evaporated.
4. In a bowl stir together mushroom mixture, parsley, and breadcrumbs. Season with salt and pepper, to taste, and cool, uncovered.
5. Preheat oven to 400-degrees.
6. On a lightly floured surface, roll out 1 pastry sheet to 14 x 10 in.
7. Halve rectangle lengthwise with a long sharp knife and spread about half of mushroom filling on 1 half, leaving a 1-inch border all around.
8. Brush edges of mushroom-topped pastry with some egg wash and put remaining pastry half on top of filling.
9. Carefully transfer empanada to a large baking sheet, leaving room for other empanadas, and brush with some remaining egg wash.
10. Make another empanada in the same manner with remaining puff pastry sheet, filling, and egg wash.
11. Put empanadas in middle of oven and reduce temperature to 375-degrees.
12. Bake empanadas until golden, about 35 minutes.

NOTE: Empanadas may be made 1 day ahead, cooled completely on a rack, wrapped in foil, and refrigerated. They can also be frozen for 2-3 months. If refrgerated, remove from the foil and heat uncovered on a baking sheet in a preheated 375-degree for about 6 minutes. If frozen, heat as described above but let them cook a little longer until browned.

SPRING GREENS WITH FRESH BERRIES, CANDIED PECANS AND BLEU CHEESE

Serving Size	6-8
Cost	$
Complexity	1.5
Pre-Prep	1 – The candied pecans can be made a day or more in advance.

Ingredients:

Salad:

Mixed Spring Greens
Crumbled Blue Cheese
Fresh Raspberries or Strawberries

Candied Pecans (see directions)
Vinaigrette (see directions)

Candied Pecans:

1/3 C Sugar
1/4 C Butter
1/4 C Orange Juice

1 1/4 t Cinnamon
3/4 t Salt
1-2 t Cayenne Pepper

Vinaigrette Salad Dressing:

1/2 C Olive Oil
1 t Shallots, minced
3 T Balsamic Vinegar (1/2 C)

1/4 t Salt
1/8 t White Pepper

Directions:

Candied Pecans

1. On medium heat, warm sugar, butter, OJ & spices.
2. When butter is melted, toss in nuts, and stir and flip around pan to cook evenly for about 5 to 10 minutes.
3. Spread the pecans on a lined cookie sheet covered with parchment paper and allow them to cool.

NOTE: They will store for weeks in an airtight container.

Salad

1. Portion spring greens on plates.
2. Add cubed pears.
3. Sprinkle with crumbled blue cheese and candied pecans.
4. Top with salad dressing and serve.

GRILLED SWORDFISH WITH MAÎTRE D'HÔTEL BUTTER

Serving Size	6-8
Cost	$$
Complexity	1 / 2 – You do need to know how to grill so this may be a "2" if you do not.
Pre-Prep	1 – The Maître d'hôtel butter can be made up to 6 months in advance if kept in an air-tight bag (with the air removed).
Wine Pairing	A Gruner Veltliner pairs well with the char from the grill and the creamy texture of the butter.

Ingredients:

Maître d'hôtel Butter:

1 C Butter
5 T Fresh Parsley, chopped
1 t Lemon Peel, freshly grated

1/4 C Fresh Lemon Juice
5-6 Dashes of Tabasco

Swordfish Steaks:

6-8 (6 oz.) Swordfish Steaks, 1 inch thick

6-8 oz. t Maître d'hôtel Butter

Directions:

Prepare Maître d'hôtel Butter:

1. Mix butter ingredients until well combined.

Prepare Swordfish Steaks:

1. Preheat the grill for at least 5 minutes on high.
2. Place the swordfish on grill.
3. Sear both sides of the swordfish on the highest heat and cooking for approximately 3 to 4 minutes per side.
4. Place 1 t of Maître d'hôtel butter on each steak and allow it to melt for a minute.
5. Transfer the swordfish to the plate and serve.

NOTE: The amount of Maître d'hôtel butter we have indicated is not used in its entirety with this meal. Simply place the excess in a Ziploc bag or an airtight container and store it in your refrigerator for future use. It will keep for more than a few weeks.

WILD RICE PILAF

Serving Size	6-8
Cost	$
Complexity	1
Pre-Prep	3 – prepare and serve

Ingredients:

1/2 C Wild Rice, uncooked	2 T Olive Oil
3 C Mushrooms, sliced	Salt and Pepper to taste
2 3/4 C Vegetable Stock	1 Onion, diced
2 Celery stalks, sliced	1/3 C Fresh Parsley, chopped
3/4 C Long Grain Rice, uncooked	4 Garlic Cloves, minced
1 t Thyme	1/3 C Almonds, chopped

Directions:

1. Bring the vegetable broth to a boil in a large saucepan and add the wild rice.
2. Cook the wild rice for 35 to 40 minutes and then add the long grain rice.
3. Cover and cook for another 15 to 20 minutes, or until rice is done cooking.
4. In a large skillet, sauté the onions until onions are brown and caramelized then add garlic and sauté for another 2 to 3 minutes.
5. Add mushrooms, celery, and spices and cook for another 5 minutes, adding more oil or a little bit of broth if needed.
6. Add the cooked rice, fresh parsley, and almonds, and stir well to combine.
7. Continue to cook for a few minutes until everything is blended evenly.

GRILLED CALYPSO PINEAPPLE OVER ICE CREAM

Serving Size   6-8
Cost $
Complexity   1
Pre-Prep   2/3 – The pineapple can be cored and cut into rings
                    before hand and then cooked when dessert is to be
                    served or you can prepare and serve immediately
                    with the sauce. The sauce must be prepared and
                    served when needed.

Ingredients:

1 Pineapple, cored and cut into rings
1/2 C Light Brown Sugar, packed
1/8 C Worcestershire Sauce
1/2 C Dark Rum

1/2 C Butter, or margarine (1 stick)
1/2 C Honey
1 t Freshly Ground Black Pepper
Vanilla Ice Cream

Directions:

1. Combine the Worcestershire sauce, honey, butter, sugar, and rum in a medium saucepan and bring to a boil, stirring constantly.
2. Reduce heat and simmer for about 10 minutes or until it begins to thicken.
3. Remove the sauce from heat and allow it to cool.
4. Preheat and oil the grill.
5. Brush pineapple pieces with sauce, sprinkle with pepper, and place on grill.
6. Cook for about 5 minutes turning occasionally.
7. Surface of the pineapple should brown.
8. Remove the pineapple from the grill, top with ice cream, and the remaining sauce.
9. Sprinkle with additional pepper if desired.

Autumn Destination

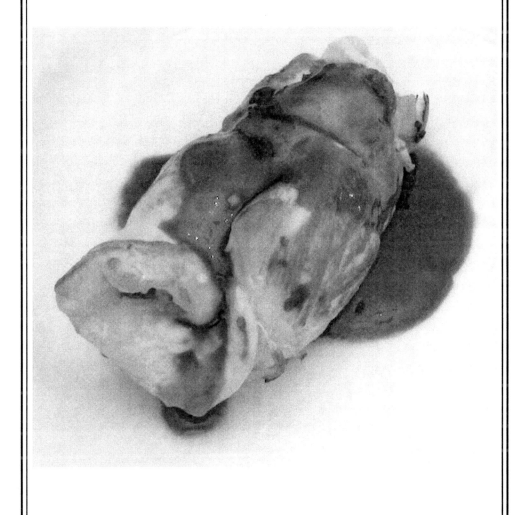

AUTUMN DESTINATION

The Autumn Destination menu is a nice transitional menu for the end of summer and the start of fall. Many of the ingredients are best found in season towards the end of the summer. Even though it may not quite be autumn, these recipes are, nonetheless, great recipes heading into the cooler nights.

The Baba Ghanouj is like hummus, only better. It takes a while to make but is worth the effort. This can be made a day in advance and refrigerated until ready to serve. The Knickerbocker Bean Soup is an extremely hearty soup that really could be served as an entire meal on a cold winter's day. Smaller portions of this soup will do well for this menu. This soup is actually two soups in one. You could, if you like, remove the carrots, tomatoes, and potatoes and serve a soup called Homestyle Bean Soup. However, given the menu pairings, we have recommended the Knickerbocker Bean Soup in this instance.

The Spinach and Feta Stuffed Chicken is far easier to prepare than the Stuffed Pork Tenderloin. Instead of cutting the chicken, we will simply pound the chicken flat like a veal scaloppini. Once flat, we will add the ingredients to the flattened chicken, roll, sear, and bake. It doesn't get much easier than that. Also, the addition of the steamed rice helps to capture the sauce the chicken is prepared with.

For dessert, we have provided a Linzer Torte. This is where the complexity of this menu lies. This dessert will take time, concentration, and effort but it will absolutely satisfy. You should double check with any potential guests that there are no known nut allergies though as this dessert incorporates several types of nuts. The Linzer Torte can be made days in advance and refrigerated.

As for the wine pairing, Donnie has recommended a Sauvignon Blanc with citrus and herbal tones.

BABA GHANOUJ

Serving Size	6-8
Cost	$
Complexity	1.5
Pre-Prep	1 – Can be made days in advance

Ingredients:

3 Med. Eggplants (about 1 pound each)
8 Garlic Cloves
1/2 C Fresh Lemon Juice

1 C Tahini, well stirred (sesame seed paste)
1/4 C Red Wine Vinegar
Olive Oil, for drizzling

Accompaniments

Pita Triangles
Bottled Pepperoncini, chopped and drained (pickled Tuscan peppers)

Onion, chopped
Kalamata Olives, chopped and pitted

Directions:

1. Preheat broiler or prepare grill.
2. Prick eggplants in several places with a fork.
3. On a broiler pan, or in a shallow baking pan, broil eggplants about 3 to 4 inches from heat, turning every 10 to 15 minutes, for 45 to 55 minutes, or until charred all over and very soft.

> *NOTE: Alternatively, you can grill eggplants on a well-oiled rack set 5 to 6 inches over glowing coals in the same manner. This can also be accomplished on a gas grill set on high.*

4. Cool the eggplants until they can be handled and peel off and discard the skin. Transfer the pulp to a colander set over a bowl.
5. Let the eggplant pulp drain for 20 minutes and discard any liquid in the bowl.
6. In a food processor, blend lemon juice, vinegar, garlic, and salt to taste until smooth.
7. Add eggplant pulp and pulse until a coarse purée.
8. Add tahini and pulse just until combined well.
9. Transfer the Baba Ghanouj to a shallow bowl and drizzle with oil.
10. Serve the Baba Ghanouj with accompaniments.

KNICKERBOCKER BEAN SOUP

Serving Size   6-8
Cost $
Complexity   1
Pre-Prep   1 – Can be made a day in advance

NOTE: Did you know that Knickerbocker Bean Soup is actually two soups in one? It's true. If you remove the carrots, diced tomatoes, and potato, you'd have soup called Homestyle Bean Soup.

Ingredients:

1/4 C Bacon, diced   1 C Potato, diced
1 Ham Hock (optional)   1 28 oz. can of Navy Beans
1 C Onion, diced   1/2 C Carrots, diced
1 16 oz. can of Diced Tomatoes   2 C Chicken Stock
1/4 C Flour

Directions:

1. In a soup pot, brown the bacon till it is evenly cooked and crispy.
2. Add the onions and cook until translucent.
3. Add flour and cook for 2 or 3 minutes.
4. Add the beans, broth, carrots, diced tomatoes, and potatoes. Then stir and let simmer for one hour.
5. If you use the ham hock, add this when the broth is added.

NOTE: When reheated, you may need to add some additional chicken stock to bring it back to the consistency of a soup. It tends to thicken when stored.

Spinach and Feta Stuffed Chicken Breasts

Serving Size	4
Cost	$
Complexity	1
Pre-Prep	2/3 – The chicken can be flattened, rolled and ready to go a few hours in advance.
Wine Pairing	A crisp Sauvignon Blanc with citrus and herbal tones will heighten the flavors of the spinach and feta in this chicken dish.

Ingredients:

4 Chicken Breasts, boneless and skinless	Salt and Freshly Ground Black Pepper
1/2 C Crumbled Feta Cheese	2 T Extra Virgin Olive Oil
1 pkg. Fresh Baby Spinach	1 C Breadcrumbs (optional)

Sauce

1/2 C Raspberry Jam	2 T Lemon Juice

Directions:

1. Place breasts in the center of a Ziplock bag or 2 large sheets of Saran Wrap.
2. Pound out the chicken from the center of the bag outward using a heavy-bottomed skillet or mallet. Be firm but controlled with your strokes.
3. Season chicken with salt and pepper
4. Lay fresh spinach in the center of the pounded chicken breast. Use at least 8 to 15 spinach leaves per chicken breast depending on the size of the spinach leaves.
5. Sprinkle Feta cheese liberally over spinach.
6. Carefully roll chicken up trying to keep spinach and feta in the middle. Use toothpicks or cooking string to hold the chicken breast together.

7. If you choose, roll the chicken breasts in breadcrumbs at this point.
8. In a sauté pan, heat 2 T of olive oil over medium heat and sear the chicken.
9. Place the seared chicken in a 350-degree oven. Roast for 25 to 30 minutes.
10. While the chicken is cooking, heat the raspberry jam and lemon juice in a small sauce pan on low to medium low heat. Stir until the jam is all liquid.
11. To serve, place a spoonful, or drizzle, of sauce on the plate and place the stuffed chicken on top.

STEAMED RICE

Serving Size   6-8
Cost $
Complexity   1
Pre-Prep   3 – Prepare and serve

Ingredients:

1 C White Long Grain Rice   2 C Water
1 T Olive Oil (or Butter)   1 t Salt

Directions:

1. Use a baking dish with good fitting lid.
2. Put rice in dish and rinse it well to wash off some of the starch. Drain.
3. Put 2 C water in dish with rice, add salt and oil.
4. Place in the oven set at 350 that has been preheated.
5. Check rice after 10 minutes and give it a stir.
6. Continue to bake for another 10 to 15 minutes.
7. Pull out of oven and let sit for 5 minutes. Serve.

LINZER TORTE

Serving Size	6-8
Cost	$
Complexity	1.5
Pre-Prep	1 – Can be made a day in advance

Ingredients:

1 C Whole Almonds (can use blanched almonds)
1/2 C Whole Hazelnuts
1 1/2 C All Purpose Flour
2/3 C Granulated White Sugar
Zest of One Lemon
1 t Ground Cinnamon
16 oz. Raspberry Preserves (High Quality Polaner Brand)

14 T Cold Unsalted Butter, cut into pieces (about two sticks)
1/4 t Salt
1/2 t Baking Powder
2 large Egg Yolks
1 t Pure Vanilla Extract
1/8 t Ground Cloves
Confectioners Sugar, for dusting (Icing or Powdered)

Directions:

1. Preheat the oven to 350-degrees with rack in the center.
2. Place almonds and hazelnuts in a food processor and process, along with 1/2 C of flour, until finely ground.
3. Add the remaining flour, sugar, lemon zest, ground cinnamon, ground cloves, salt, and baking powder and process until evenly combined.
4. Add the butter and pulse until the mixture looks like fine crumbs.
5. Add the 2 egg yolks and vanilla extract and pulse until the dough just begins to come together.
6. Gather the dough into a ball and then divide it into two pieces, one slightly larger than the other.
7. Wrap the smaller ball of dough in plastic wrap and refrigerate for about an hour or until firm enough to roll.

8. Take the larger ball of dough and press it onto the bottom and up the sides of a buttered 9-10 inch tart pan.
9. Take the cooled raspberry preserves and spread them over the bottom of the crust.
10. Cover with plastic wrap and place in the refrigerator.
11. Once the smaller ball of dough is firm, remove from the fridge and roll it between two sheets of wax paper into a circle that is about 12 inches in diameter.
12. Using a pastry wheel or pizza cutter, cut the pastry into 1 inch (2.5 cm) strips.
13. When strips are firm, using an offset spatula, gently and carefully transfer the strips to the tart pan.
14. Lay half the strips, evenly spaced, across the torte and then turn the pan a quarter turn and lay the remaining strips across the first strips to create a lattice.

NOTE: Don't worry if the pastry tears, just press it back together as best as you can. Trim the edges of the strips to fit the tart pan.

---

15. If you have any leftover scraps of dough, roll them into a long rope. Don't worry if the rope breaks. Just take the pieces of rope and place them around the outer edge of the tart where the end of the lattice strips meets the bottom crust.
16. Using a fork or your fingers, press the rope into the edges of the bottom crust to seal the edges.
17. Bake the tart in a preheated 350-degree oven for about 30-35 minutes or until the pastry is golden brown and set.
18. Let the torte cool on a wire rack before un-molding.

19. Dust the top of the torte with confectioners' sugar. If not serving on the same day, wait to dust before serving.

NOTE: Although you can serve this torte the same day as it is baked you can cover and store it overnight before serving. The Linzer Torte is heaven when served warm with a dollop of whipped cream. However, the torte will keep for a few days at room temperature or in the refrigerator for about a week. It can also be frozen.

Provencal Summer

PROVENCAL SUMMER

Believe it or not, the inspiration for this menu came to me while wandering through our local grocery store. I found the basis for the main course in a local wine magazine called *The Wine Buzz*. It's a free publication for marketing local/regional vineyards, beers, and tastings among other things. Occasionally, they print a recipe or two to provide examples of good wine pairings. I converted the Provencal Pistou Pasta recipe for family one summer, coupled it with the Fresh Corn Salad, and it was devoured!

Another variation I like to utilize involves fresh sautéed zucchini and squash. The incorporation of the zucchini and squash adds a touch of seasonal ingredients and some additional color. Not to mention a unique flavor.

The Olive Tapenade will get the food processor warmed up as all of the ingredients are added to the processor and mixed to create a very Mediterranean style spread. Use some creativity for the accompaniments in which to place the Tapenade. Scott prefers his Olive Tapenade with anchovies and capers while I prefer to leave the anchovies out. We would recommend making a batch sometime prior to the event so you can decide for yourself if the like the saltiness of the anchovies or not.

The Provencal Pistou Pasta also requires some processor work as everything but the cream and the linguine are mixed together to form the Pistou Sauce. The Pistou Sauce is like a Pesto sauce but not nearly as heavy or thick. The addition of the diced Roma tomatoes will add some color to this creamy pasta dish.

My girls have coined this dish the "Yummy Pasta." Do yourself a favor and stack all of the fresh basil leaves together on top of one another. Once stacked, roll them up like a cigar, and then chiffonade cut them into ribbons before placing them into the mini Quizinart. One of the reasons that Provencal Pistou Pasta is so delicious is the chiffonade cutting of the fresh basil prior to blending. By performing the chiffonade cut, you are releasing the sweeter aspects of the fresh basil. Without the chiffonade cut, the pasta dish takes on a more pungent clove taste. My daughters have mistaken this pungency for spiciness, of which, there is none in the dish.

To complete this menu offering, add a helping of the Fresh Corn Salad to the plate. The Fresh Corn Salad utilizes a cider vinegar that, combined with the ribbons of fresh basil, complements the Provencal Pistou Pasta extremely well.

In keeping with the Provencal theme, we have provided an extremely easy to prepare Simple Wildberry Shortbread recipe that finishes off the menu. Brambles and wild berries abound in the south of France so this complements the menu nicely.

Donnie has provided us with a red and a white wine pairing for this menu depending on your tastes and preferences. For the red lovers, he has selected a Grenache-based Cotes du Rhone, or if you prefer white, try the fruity Chenin Blanc.

OLIVE TAPENADE

Serving Size	6-8
Cost	$
Complexity	1
Pre-Prep	1 / 2 – This can be made a few hours, or even a day, in advance and refrigerated.

Ingredients:

1 Clove Garlic, chopped

1 t Fresh Thyme, chopped

1 3/4 C Whole Kalamata Olives, pitted

1 t Fresh Rosemary, chopped

2 T Capers

3 T Lemon Juice

1 (2 oz.) Can of Anchovy Fillets, rinsed

4 T Olive Oil

NOTE: Most grocers carry tubes of anchovy paste. If available in your area, this ingredient can be replaced with 2 T of anchovy paste.

Directions:

1. Combine garlic, olives, anchovies, capers, thyme, rosemary, and lemon juice in a food processor.
2. Slowly drip the olive oil into the food processor while you are blending the ingredients together.
3. Great served with pita chips.

PROVENCAL PISTOU PASTA

Serving Size	6-8
Cost	$
Complexity	1
Pre-Prep	3 – Prepare and serve
Wine Pairing	The rustic edge of a Grenache-based Cotes du Rhone red is the perfect accompaniment to this dish. If you prefer white, try the fruit-forward flavors of a Chenin Blanc.

Ingredients:

1 (16 oz) Linguine
1 C Grated Parmesan
2 T Butter
1 Small Container of Heavy Cream
4 Garlic Cloves, peeled

3 Roma Tomatoes, diced
1/4 t Sea Salt
Grated Parmesan for garnish
1/4 C Extra Virgin Olive Oil, preferably from Provencal region
2 C Fresh Basil (about 15 leaves)

Directions:

1. Begin cooking the linguine as directed.
2. While the pasta is cooking, begin preparing the Pistou mixture by adding the heavy cream to a medium sized sauté pan over low heat. If the cream forms a skin, the heat is too high.
3. Mince garlic and salt in a food processor.
4. Stack and chiffonade cut the basil then add the basil ribbons and 1/2 C cheese and mix until well blended.
5. Scrape down sides of bowl.
6. Run processor on low and slowly add the olive oil until well blended.
7. Stir the Pistou mixture from the processor into the warming cream.
8. When the pasta is al dente, drain but reserve 1/2 C of pasta water.

9. Place the cooked linguine, and the reserved pasta water, in a large serving bowl and stir in the butter. Keep warm.
10. Pour the Pistou mixture over linguine and garnish with diced tomatoes and 1/2 C additional Parmesan cheese. Stir well to incorporate all ingredients.

> *NOTE: The Parmesan cheese garnish will thicken the sauce. Use as little or as much as you like.*

FRESH CORN SALAD

Serving Size	6-8
Cost	$
Complexity	1
Pre-Prep	1 & 2 - The Fresh Corn Salad can be made a day in advance or even a few hours. It is best when cold.

Ingredients:

5 Ears of Corn, shucked
3 T Good Olive Oil
3 Roma Tomatoes, sliced and quartered
1 8" Cucumber, peeled, sliced, and quartered
3 T Cider Vinegar

1/2 t Fresh Ground Black Pepper
1/2 t Kosher Salt
1/4 C Small-Diced Red Onion (about 1 small onion)
1/2 C Julienne Cut Fresh Basil Leaves (do not tear basil by hand)

Directions:

1. In a large pot of boiling salted water, cook the corn for 3 minutes until the starchiness is just gone.
2. Drain and immerse it in ice water to stop the cooking and to set the color.
3. When the corn is cool, cut the kernels off the cob, cutting close to the cob.
4. Toss the kernels in a large bowl with the tomato, red onions, vinegar, cucumber, olive oil, salt, and pepper.
5. Just before serving toss in the fresh basil.
6. Taste for seasonings and serve cold or at room temperature.

SIMPLE WILDBERRY SHORTBREAD

Serving Size	6-8
Cost	$
Complexity	1
Pre-Prep	2 – Can be made a few hours ahead and refrigerated before cooking.

Ingredients:

1 3 lb. bag Frozen Triple Berry Blend (raspberries, blueberries, blackberries)
1/2 Stick of Butter

1 box of Shortbread Cookies (crumbled)

Directions:

1. Pour frozen berries into 9 x 11 baking dish - preferably glass.
2. Sprinkle crumbled cookies over top, covering the berries evenly.
3. Place sliced pats of butter on top of crumbles spreading out evenly to distribute butter throughout the dish.
4. Bake at 350-degrees until berries start to bubble on the sides.
5. Remove from oven and let it set up for 30 to 45 minutes.
6. Serve with ice cream on top.

A Peppery Debate

A PEPPERY DEBATE

Scott and I have conflicting opinions regarding the choice in peppercorn for Steak Au Poivre. I prefer my peppercorn robust and strong. Hence, black peppercorn. Scott prefers the milder notes generally associated with the green peppercorn. As a result, we had a bit of pepper debate regarding this menu offering. In the end, Scott relented, probably out of humility for having won all of the other debates while writing this book. However, something we both agree on is the need for a digital instant read thermometer. You will be checking several pieces of meat that are cooking and warming at different rates, as a result, we felt it important enough to point this out.

The reason the meat will cook and warm at different rates has more to do with the thickness of the meat than their locations in the oven but both are factors. Therefore, a digital instant read thermometer is a wise investment for this menu, and in general. Also, as we discussed in the Inner Chef chapter, a good cook must learn how to determine when something is done by means other than sight. This can be temperature or touch.

As for the menu as a whole, it has a "surf and turf" quality to it. First, we start you off with the Shrimp Gabriella, which is a straightforward stuffed and wrapped shrimp that can be prepared and served inside of fifteen minutes. Then you and your guests can enjoy a Tomato Basil

Mozzarella Salad and Balsamic Vinaigrette. This salad is presented differently than your traditional salad in that the ribbons of basil represent the only "greens" in the salad, which is part of the dressing. The salad also carries over the Prosciutto ingredient found in the Shrimp Gabriella.

The Steak Au Poivre recipe we have provided here was inspired by yet another grocery store excursion when I picked up a publication while walking through the store. The recipe itself may intimidate you, due to the number of steps, but it is actually quite easy to prepare. The tart cherry and port sauce coupled with the starchiness of the Roasted Red Potatoes will have your taste buds hopping all through the main course. For dessert, we carry over the port ingredient from the Steak Au Poivre and create a Poached Pears in Port dish that can be prepared and refrigerated days in advance.

For this menu, Donnie has given us two wines to choose from. So, depending on how wide your adventurous spirit is, you could go with either a Cabernet Sauvignon or try a Syrah. The tannins in the Cabernet go well with high protein dishes and is a safe selection. The Syrah, however, turns the grape varieties found in the syrah and port against each other for a little battle of the vines in your mouth.

SHRIMP GABRIELLA

Serving Size	6-8
Cost	$
Complexity	1 / 2 (depends on your grilling skills)
Pre-Prep	2 – You can stuff and wrap the shrimp a few hours ahead without any reservations. Keep refrigerated until ready to cook.

Ingredients:

12 Large Shrimp (or Prawns)
6 slices Prosciutto
6 oz. Provolone Cheese, cut into
12 strips

1/4 C Barbecue Sauce
1/4 C Green Chile Peppers, diced

Directions:

1. Peel, de-vein, and butterfly the shrimp, or prawns. (To butterfly shrimp, split the shrimp down the center, where the vein was, cutting almost completely through.)
2. Insert a strip of provolone cheese and 1 t of the diced green chilies into each shrimp.
3. Fold over the shrimp and wrap with Prosciutto.
4. Secure with wooden picks.
5. Cook the shrimp on the grill on medium heat, basting with your favorite barbecue sauce, until bacon is cooked and shrimp is pink.

Tomato Basil Mozzarella Salad and Balsamic Vinaigrette

Serving Size	6-8
Cost	$
Complexity	1
Pre-Prep	2 – You can prepare the plates with the alternating tomato mozzarella presentation and refrigerate until ready to serve. Reserve the dressing until you serve though.

Ingredients:

1/2 C Balsamic Vinegar
8 oz. Mozzarella (preferably the curd type found as balls in liquid)
1 1/2 C Extra Virgin Olive Oil
2 t Garlic, chopped
1 Bunch of Fresh Basil

8 slices Prosciutto
1 T Red Onion or Shallot, chopped
Salt and Pepper to taste
5 Tomatoes, large and ripe

Directions:

1. Put vinegar in a bowl, and add 6 basil leaves cut chiffonade style (means thinly sliced).
2. While whisking rapidly, slowly add the olive oil.
3. Add salt and pepper to taste.
4. Slice tomatoes very thin - approximately 7 slices per tomato, excluding the end pieces.
5. Slice mozzarella into pieces the same thickness and approximately half the size of the tomato slices.
6. On a plate, going in a circle, alternate the tomato and mozzarella slices all the way around the plate.

7. Five minutes before serving, whisk the dressing briefly to incorporate.
8. Spoon the dressing over the salads.
9. Finally, place 2 slices of prosciutto in the center of the plate, scrunching them some for height.
10. Add fresh ground black pepper on top and serve.

Steak Au Poivre

Serving Size	4-6
Cost	$ / $$
Complexity	1 / 2
Pre-Prep	2 – The steaks need to tenderize prior to being seared and baked.
Wine Pairing	The dark fruits and tannins in a Cabernet Sauvignon will pair nicely with the meaty texture and proteins found in the beef. For the more adventurous, try a Syrah. The Syrah will pit the grape's peppery notes head to head with the Port of the pan sauce.

Ingredients:

1 8"-10" long piece of Center Cut Beef Tenderloin cut to allow a 1 1/2" - 2" thick steak for each guest

NOTE: Or if you prefer, instead of a whole tenderloin, purchase 6-8 pcs. of pre-cut 2" thick Filet Mignon from your grocers meat counter.

Peppercorn Seasoning

5 T Cracked Black Peppercorn   1 T Salt
5 T Olive Oil (+ an additional 2 T to sear)

NOTE: 2 1/2 – 3 T whole peppercorn = approximately 5 T cracked. Also, a digital instant read thermometer is highly recommended.

Pan Sauce

2 C Port	1 Sprig of Thyme
1/2 T Balsamic Vinegar	1 C Dried Tart Cherries
1 T Shallot, minced	1 T Butter

Directions:

1. Cut the tenderloin into 1 1/2" - 2" thick steaks, one for each guest.
2. Using the back of a skillet, crack the 2 1/2 – 3 T of black peppercorn to make 5 T of cracked black peppercorn.
3. Place 5 T Olive Oil in a pan and add the cracked peppercorn.
4. Over medium heat, let it barely simmer for 7-10 minutes until you start to smell aromatic things like floral notes, or coffee, or chocolate. (I smelled the floral notes last time I prepared this.)
5. Pour the peppercorn and oil mixture into a bowl, add the salt, and mix well.
6. Coat the meat with the peppercorn mixture, cover, and let sit on a wire rack on the counter for an hour. This will tenderize the meat. Place a plate or a pan under the wire rack to catch any juices.
7. With 15 minutes left on the tenderizing step, in a separate pan, combine the port, vinegar, thyme, cherries and shallot and let reduce on a slight simmer for about 30 minutes, stirring often.
8. While the pan sauce is reducing, pre-heat a sheet pan in the oven at 450-degrees. (You'll be placing the seared beef on this pan.)
9. Place 2 T of oil in a cold pan and turn the burner on high to quickly heat the pan. Once hot, turn the heat down to medium high heat. The olive oil will smoke slightly when the pan is ready.
10. Using tongs to preserve the peppercorn crust, place the tenderloin gently in the pan with plenty of room in the pan between pieces - this is for more even heating.
11. Sear the tenderloin pieces for 3-4 minutes on each side (top and bottom only).

12. Use the tongs to preserve the peppercorn crust and place the steaks in the oven on the pre-heated sheet pan and cook for 5-7 minutes until the steak reaches an approximate internal temperature of 115 – 120-degrees.
13. Remove the tenderloin from the oven and place on the previously used wire rack over a baking sheet or plate to rest for 5-10 minutes. The internal temperature will continue to rise approximately 10-degrees in that time, leaving you with a 125 – 130-degree internal temperature, which is medium rare.

> *NOTE: If you do not like your meat that rare, let it reach 125-degrees before removing it from the oven. You'll be near "medium" after the cooling step.*

14. After the tenderloin has rested for the appropriate amount of time, add 1 T of butter to the pan sauce that has been reducing and whisk until melted and incorporated.
15. To serve, either slice the tenderloin pieces and place on the plate covering with a spoonful or two of the pan sauce over top –OR- place the entire tenderloin (uncut) on the plate and covering with a spoonful or two of the port sauce.

ROASTED RED POTATOES

Serving Size	6-8
Cost	$
Complexity	1
Pre-Prep	2 – The potatoes can be cut and ready to go hours before the event.

Ingredients:

8 Red Potatoes (medium sized potatoes)   2 T Olive Oil
1 T Kosher Salt

Directions:

1. Wash and cut potatoes.
2. Coat potatoes with olive oil.
3. Sprinkle kosher salt over potatoes.
4. Roast in roasting pan in a 400-degree oven for 35 to 40 minutes.
5. Serve warm.

POACHED PEARS IN PORT

Serving Size	4-6 – the pears can be split among guests if you like but the recipe calls for only 4 pears.
Cost	$
Complexity	1.5
Pre-Prep	1 – Can be made a day or two in advance.

Ingredients:

4 C Port
1 Stick Cinnamon, 2 in. long
1 C Water
1 t Allspice, whole
1 Vanilla Bean, split lengthwise and scraped, seeds and pod reserved

1/8 t Kosher Salt
Zest of 1 Lemon
1/2 C Granulated Sugar
4 Firm Bosc or Anjou Pears (about 1 pound)

Directions:

1. Combine all ingredients, except pears, in a medium sized saucepan and bring to a boil over high heat, stirring until sugar dissolved.
2. Meanwhile, peel pears, leaving the stems intact.
3. Slice off the bottom 1/8 inch of each pear to create a flat and stable base.
4. Reduce heat to keep poaching liquid at a bare simmer and add pears, laying them on their sides so that they are almost completely submerged.
5. Cook the pears, turning occasionally, so that they become saturated on all sides, until they are just tender when pierced with a fork, about 7 minutes.
6. Allow pears to cool completely in the poaching liquid.
7. Serve or transfer pears and liquid to an airtight container and store in the refrigerator for up to 2 days.

Northern Exposure

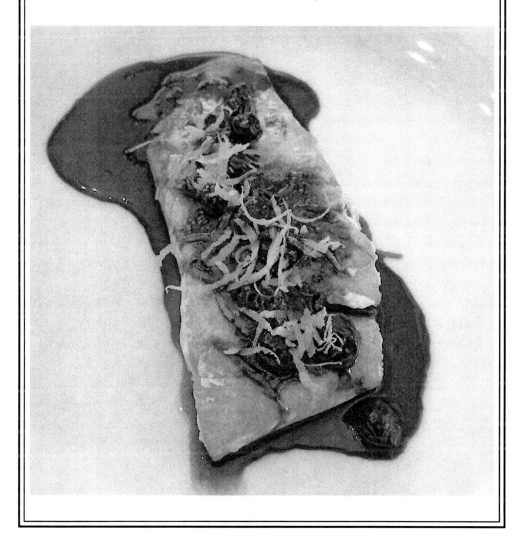

Northern Exposure

This menu has an over-arching fruit theme that is applicable to four of the five noted recipes. Between these four dishes, you will enjoy oranges, blueberries, raisins, and raspberries respectively.

We start you off fairly easily with two simple dishes in the Bruschetta and the salad. However, the menu becomes more difficult once you begin the main dish and dessert.

The five minutes in the Five-Minute Bruschetta alludes to the amount of time it takes to make this appetizer. Simply take all of the ingredients, except for the bread, mix them together, top the bread with the mixture, and bake.

The Mandarin Mixed Green Salad is also just a simple. For the salad, simply combine the vinaigrette dressing ingredients, then combine the greens and oranges, coat the greens and oranges with the dressing, and then garnish with the remaining ingredients.

The Pan Seared Salmon with Blueberry Glaze is a heavenly and fruity concoction that is balanced nicely against the mild heat of the Spiced Quinoa Tembales. The Quinoa aids the dinner by absorbing some of the blueberry glaze.

As for the wine pairing, Donnie has provided us with an unoaked Chardonnay to play with the glaze of the salmon.

For dessert, we hide a little sugary goodness inside individual cakes that make up the Chocolate Molten Bombe with Raspberries recipe. With each bite, you receive either a fruity surprise in the raspberries or a little kiss of chocolate, or both.

FIVE-MINUTE BRUSCHETTA

Serving Size	6-8
Cost	$
Complexity	1
Pre-Prep	2 - The Bruschetta mixture can be prepared a few hours ahead of time.

Ingredients:

2 Large Tomatoes, coarsely chopped
8 oz. Mozzarella, grated
1/2 C Capers (Optional)
1/2 Sweet Onion, chopped
1 Loaf Italian or French bread, cut into 1 in. slices

1/4 C Parmesan Cheese, freshly grated
1 t Fresh Basil, chopped
2 T Olive Oil
4 Cloves Garlic, minced (Optional)
1/4 lb. Pepperoni, thin sliced (Optional)

Directions:

1. Preheat oven to 400-degrees.
2. In a medium bowl, combine tomatoes, onion, Mozzarella, olive oil, and basil.
3. Place bread on a baking sheet, and top with tomato mixture.
4. Sprinkle with Parmesan.
5. Bake in preheated oven for 8 to 10 minutes, or until bottom of bread is browned.
6. Allow to cool for 5 minutes before serving.

MANDARIN MIXED GREEN SALAD

Serving Size   Serves 4-6
Cost $
Complexity   1
Pre-Prep   2 - Do not add dressing until ready to serve.

Ingredients:

Salad

4 C Mixed Salad Greens, torn
1 Avocado, sliced
1 C Mandarin Oranges

8 Grape Tomatoes
1/2 C Chopped Walnuts, toasted
Red Onion, thinly sliced (optional)

Citrus Vinaigrette

3 T Orange Juice
1 t Dijon Mustard
2 t Balsamic Vinegar
1 Garlic Clove, minced

1 t Olive Oil
1 t Soy Sauce, reduced sodium
1 t Honey
1/2 t Gingerroot, minced via garlic press

Directions:

1. In a dressing container, combine all vinaigrette ingredients and shake vigorously.
2. Place greens and oranges in a bowl and toss with vinaigrette.
3. Divide the salad onto two plates and garnish with walnuts, avocado, tomatoes, and onions.

PAN SEARED SALMON W/ BLUEBERRY GLAZE

Serving Size	4-6
Cost	$ / $$
Complexity	1.5
Pre-Prep	3 - must be prepared and served immediately
Wine Pairing	An unoaked Chardonnay has bright fruit flavors and some acidity to play with the makeup of this delicious glaze.

Ingredients:

1 lb. Fresh, Wild Alaskan Salmon, cut into 4-6 equal medium steak sized pieces
1/2 C Pomegranate Juice
1/4 C Balsamic Vinegar
1 T Extra Virgin Olive Oil

1/4 C Sugar In The Raw (also referred to as turbinado sugar – this is not brown sugar)
1 t Lemon Zest
1 C Fresh Blueberries
Kosher Salt & Fresh Cracked Black Pepper, taste

Directions:

Blueberry Balsamic Glaze

1. Pour pomegranate juice, balsamic vinegar, and turbinado sugar into a large sauté pan and heat on high.
2. Cook 4-6 minutes, stirring constantly.
3. Once sauce starts to thicken, add blueberries, salt and pepper.
4. Cook an additional 2-3 minutes until it's the consistency of maple syrup. Set aside.

Salmon

1. Season salmon filets with salt and pepper.
2. Heat oil in a large sauté pan over medium-high heat.
3. Place salmon in hot oil, skin-side up, and cook for 4 minutes.
4. Flip and cook an additional 4 minutes, or until the internal temperature reaches 145-degrees.
5. Place salmon on a serving dish and top with blueberry balsamic glaze.
6. Garnish with lemon zest.

SPICED QUINOA TIMBALES

Serving Size	4-6
Cost	$
Complexity	1
Pre-Prep	3 - Prepare and serve immediately

Ingredients:

1 C Quinoa	1 t Ground Cumin
1 C Chicken Stock	1/2 t Cinnamon
1 Small Onion, minced	1/2 t Salt
2/3 C Water	1/4 t Turmeric
1 T Olive Oil	3 T Fresh Parsley, finely chopped
1/3 C Dried Currants, or raisins	1/4 C Canned Tomatoes, chopped & drained

Directions:

1. In a fine sieve, rinse the quinoa under cold water for 1 minute and drain it well.
2. In a heavy saucepan cook the onion in the oil over moderately low heat, stirring, until it is softened, add the cumin, the cinnamon, and the turmeric, and cook the mixture, stirring, for 30 seconds.
3. Add the quinoa and cook the mixture, stirring, for 1 minute.
4. Add the broth, the water, the currants, the tomatoes, and the salt and simmer the mixture, covered, for 15 minutes, or until the liquid is absorbed.
5. Remove the pan from the heat, let the mixture stand, covered, for 5 minutes, and stir in the parsley.
6. Divide the quinoa mixture among 6 buttered 1/2-C timbale molds, or Ccake pan, packing it, and invert the timbales onto a platter.

CHOCOLATE MOLTEN BOMBE WITH RASPBERRIES

Serving Size	6-8
Cost	$
Complexity	1
Pre-Prep	3 – prepare and serve

Ingredients:

3/4 C Granulated Sugar
1/2 C Butter, softened (1 stick)   10 Hershey Kisses
1/4 t Salt   1 t Vanilla Extract
2 Eggs, large   1 C Flour
1 1/2 C Fresh Raspberries   Powdered sugar (optional)
2 T Cocoa Powder (remove for   1/3 C Evaporated Milk (1/4 C for
white cake)   white cake)

Directions:

1. Preheat the oven to 350-degrees.
2. Grease 10 muffin C or use silicone muffin
3. Beat granulated sugar and butter in large mixer bowl until combined.
4. Add eggs, evaporated milk, and vanilla extract; beat until blended.
5. Stir in flour and salt.
6. Gently fold in raspberries.
7. Spoon heaping T batter into each prepared C; place 1 bite-size chocolate in each C, pressing down slightly.
8. Spoon heaping T batter over each chocolate, covering completely.
9. Bake for 20 to 22 minutes or until cakes are golden brown around edges and top is set.
10. Cool in pan on wire rack for 10 minutes.
11. Run knife around edges to loosen; gently invert onto serving plate.
12. Sprinkle with powdered sugar; serve warm with fresh raspberry garnish.

Herb Garden

HERB GARDEN

This menu contains so many earthy items in the form of bulbs and herbs it was difficult to come up with a better menu name. To give you some idea as to what you are headed toward with this menu selection, the Herb Garden menu incorporates rosemary, chives, scallions, shallots, fennel, cilantro, parsley, garlic, tarragon, and red pepper. Your taste buds will be so worked up by the end of it all that the dessert of Chocolate Covered Strawberries will be welcome respite.

The Rosemary Peasant Bread was discovered on an outing during a Midwestern blizzard. My wife grew up in the Midwest and was use to such conditions. I, on the other hand, get positively giddy with excitement when it snows and feel an almost primal urge to go drive in it. I attended college in the mountains of North Carolina so, from my perspective, the driving wasn't that bad. My wife and children had the day off from school, due to a snowstorm, so they drove through the storm to meet me for lunch. We chose to meet at restaurant near my office, which consequently, is also near the mall. Their real purpose for the visit was eventually revealed over this delicious bread. Once we were seated, the waiter brought out this warm bread that was absolutely to die for. I'm a huge carb junkie, what can I say!

Anyway, since I have a natural proclivity to be curious, I inquired about the bread. They told me, much to my amazement, that they are provided this delicious bread in the form of a dough ball. They only bake it in the restaurant. What abject horror. They did tell me, however, that it was called "Rosemary Peasant Bread," so of course I went back to office and looked for it online. I amended the recipe I found but chose the recipe I did because it is the simplest and requires no kneading!

During the course of helping Scott organize his life in terms of the thousands of recipes he possesses, I stumbled upon this little gem of a recipe in the Braised Halibut. As I noted earlier, for reasons unknown, I have been fascinated with France, the French people, their history, and the Provence region (southern France) in particular. So this recipe was of great interest to me. When my wife was informed of what I would be serving for dinner, she promptly found a Cilantro Rice recipe and I served the Braised Halibut Provencal over Cilantro Rice.

After consuming the bread, halibut, and rice, you will definitely feel like you just took a leisurely stroll through someone's garden because of all the fresh herbs and bulb vegetables you will use. Also, the Gazpacho works well to set up the flavors of the Braised Halibut Provencal and the Cilantro Rice.

During the course of preparing the meal, I conferred with Scott regarding the size of the fennel bulb. I didn't feel that I needed that much fennel.

He replied that "Yes, I needed it" and that the fennel "adds a licorice note to the dish." I can say that it definitely smelled like licorice as I was chopping it but its potency was downgraded during the baking. It actually was a nice touch.

Donnie has provided us with a White Burgundy (Chardonnay) to enjoy with this dish. Ask your wine store for one that contains "little or no oak" as Donnie is selecting this wine because it has the punch to mingle with this flavorful French dish.

ROSEMARY PEASANT BREAD

Serving Size	6-8
Cost	$
Complexity	1
Pre-Prep	2 / 3 - This bread can be made a few hours ahead but is best when served warm.

Ingredients:

1 Packet Dry Yeast (or 2 1/2 t)

2 C Warm Water

1 T Sugar

4 C Flour

2 t Sea Salt (for dough)

3 T Fresh Rosemary, finely chopped (for dough)

1 T Olive Oil

1 T Corn Meal

2 T Butter, melted

1 T Sea Salt (for topping)

1 1/2 T Fresh Rosemary, coarsely chopped (for topping)

Directions:

1. Dissolve yeast in the warm water and sugar.
2. Add flour, 2 t sea salt, and 3 T Rosemary and stir until blended. Do not knead the dough.
3. Cover with a moist towel and let rise for 1 hour or until double in size.
4. Lightly coat a cookie sheet in olive oil and sprinkled with corn meal on top of the oil.
5. Remove the dough by dividing it into two loaves (rounds). It will be extremely sticky.
6. Place the 2 loaves on the cookie sheet and cover with the wet towel, or greased plastic wrap, and then let it rise another hour.
7. Brush each round with melted butter and lightly sprinkle with more 1 1/2 T of Rosemary and 1 T sea salt.
8. Bake at 425-degrees for 10 minutes, then reduce temp to 375-degrees for 20-25 minutes more (until the top is golden brown).

GAZPACHO

Serving Size   6-8
Cost $
Complexity   1
Pre-Prep   1 - Make a day in advance.

Ingredients:

6 Ripe Tomatoes, peeled and chopped
2 T Lemon Juice, freshly squeezed
1 Purple Onion, finely chopped
2 t Sugar
1 Cucumber, peeled, seeded, and chopped
Salt and Fresh Ground Pepper, to taste
2 T Fresh Chives, chopped

1 t Worcestershire Sauce (omit for vegetarian option)
1 Clove Garlic, minced
2 C Chicken Stock
1-2 T Fresh Parsley, chopped
6+ Drops of Tabasco Sauce, to taste
1 Sweet Green Bell Pepper (or red), seeded and chopped
2 C V-8 Juice

Directions:

1. Combine all ingredients.
2. Blend slightly, to desired consistency and place in non-metal, non-reactive storage container.
3. Cover tightly and refrigerate overnight, allowing flavors to blend.

BRAISED HALIBUT PROVENCAL

Serving Size	4
Cost	$
Complexity	1
Pre-Prep	3 – Prepare and serve
Wine Pairing	A vibrant White Burgundy (Chardonnay) with little or no oak has the punch to mingle with this flavorful French dish.

Ingredients:

3 T Extra Virgin Olive Oil
1/2 C White Wine
1 Clove Garlic, minced
12 Black Olives, pitted/sliced
1/4 t Dried Red Pepper Flakes
4 (4-5 oz.) portions Halibut
1 14-oz Can Diced Tomatoes, with juice

1/2 t Salt
1 Fennel Bulb, chopped
1/4 t Black Pepper
1/2 C Green Bell Pepper, diced
1 T Fresh Tarragon, chiffonade
2 Shallots, sliced

Directions:

1. Preheat oven to 400-degrees.
2. Heat the olive oil in a deep ovenproof skillet over medium heat, and sauté the garlic and red pepper flakes for about 20 seconds.
3. Add the shallots and fennel; cook for 3 minutes.
4. Add the diced tomatoes and white wine.
5. Simmer for 3-5 minutes until fennel is tender and liquid reduced.
6. Remove from heat and stir in the olives.
7. Salt and pepper the halibut and arrange over mixture in skillet.
8. Bake in preheated oven for 15-18 minutes or until fish is cooked through (140-degrees).
9. Stir the tarragon chiffonade into the hot vegetable mixture and serve.

CILANTRO RICE

Serving Size   6-8
Cost $
Complexity   1
Pre-Prep   2 / 3 - Can be made a few hours in advance but you should time the halibut and rice to finished at the same time.

Ingredients:

White Rice

For each C of uncooked rice:

2/3 C Cilantro, loosely packed   1 T Fresh Lime Juice
1/4 C Scallions, chopped   1 t Olive Oil
1/2 C Onion (whatever type is handy), chopped

Directions:

1. Cook rice as usual with 1 t salt per C of rice.
2. Using a mini-Quizinart, blend all remaining ingredients.
3. Once the rice is finished cooking, add the blended ingredients, mix well and serve.

CHOCOLATE COVERED STRAWBERRIES

Serving Size   As Needed
Cost $
Complexity   1
Pre-Prep   1 / 2 – Can be made a day or a few hours in advance. The chocolate needs time to harden appropriately.

Ingredients:

6 oz. Semisweet Chocolate   3 oz. White Chocolate
1 lb. Strawberries, with stems
(about 20)

Directions:

1. Put the semisweet and white chocolates into 2 separate heatproof medium bowls.
2. Fill medium saucepan with a couple inches of water and bring to a simmer over medium heat.
3. Turn off the heat; set the bowl of chocolate over the water to melt.
4. Stir until smooth.

NOTE: Melt the white chocolate in a microwave at half power, for 1 minute, stir and then heat for another minute or until melted.

5. Once the chocolates are melted and smooth, remove from the heat.
6. Line a sheet pan with parchment or waxed paper.
7. Holding the strawberry by the stem, dip the fruit into the dark chocolate, lift and twist slightly, letting any excess chocolate fall back into the bowl.
8. Set strawberries on the parchment paper.
9. Repeat with the rest of the strawberries.
10. Dip a fork in the white chocolate and drizzle the white chocolate over the dipped strawberries.
11. Set the strawberries aside until the chocolate sets, about 30 minutes.

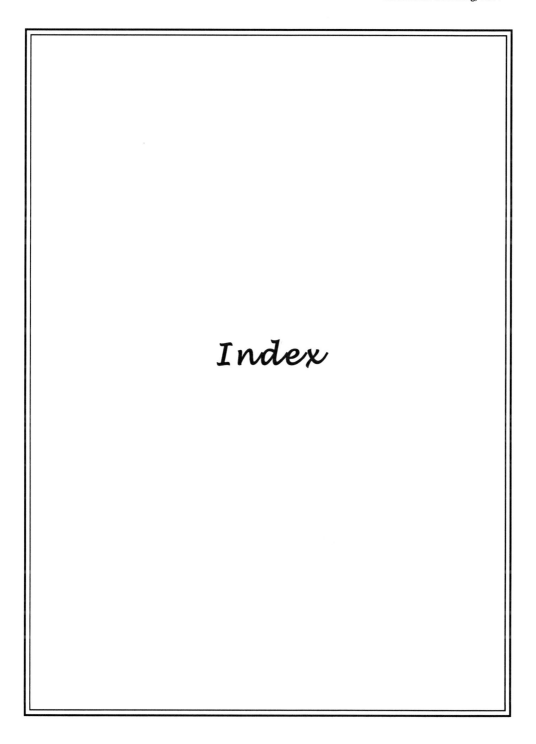

Index

INDEX

COMING
FALL 2012

Just a Small Gathering, Volume II

Back to Kitchen Basics

In *Just a Small Gathering, Volume I*, we discussed the basics of informal event planning and the aspects associated with accomplishing a comfortable and relaxing gathering of family and friends. *Just a Small Gathering, Volume II* will prepare you to become the best cook you can be.

Volume II provides all of the background material needed to generate and enhance your efficiency in the kitchen. We continue several discussions we began in *Volume I* as we strive to increase your skills and build upon the foundation of several key concepts. And lastly, we have provided the essential recipes needed to make the best stocks, soups, sauces, sautés, and grilled items.

Look for *Volume II* in the Fall of 2012...

CPSIA information can be obtained at www.ICGtesting.com
Printed in the USA
LVOW021744100112

262942LV00004B/1/P